I HAVE

issues

JELLY VALIMONT

I HAVE
issues

JELLY VALIMONT

BLAZE
PUBLISHING
MANSFIELD, TEXAS

I HAVE ISSUES
by Jelly Valimont

Published by Blaze Publishing House
www.blazepublishinghouse.com
BPH is a division of Ministry Solutions, LLC
P.O. Box 184
Mansfield, TX 76063
817.473.9704

Unless otherwise noted, all Scripture quotations are from the NEW AMERICAN STANDARD–UDATED VERSION of the Bible. Copyright © 1960, 1962, 1963, 1968, 1971, 1972, 1973, 1975, 1977 by the Lockman Foundation. Used by permission.

Scripture quotations noted KJV are taken from the KING JAMES VERSION of the Bible. Copyright © 1979, 1980, 1982 by Thomas Nelson, Inc., Publishers. Used by permission.

Scripture quotations noted NKJV are taken from the NEW KING JAMES VERSION. Copyright © 1979, 1980, 1982, Thomas Nelson, Inc., Publishers.

Scripture quotations noted TLB are taken from THE LIVING BIBLE. Copyright © 1971. Used by permission of Tyndale House Publishers, Inc., Wheaton, Illinois 60189.

Scripture quotations marked NLT are taken from the NEW LIVING TRANSLATION. Copyright © 1996. Used by permission of Tyndale House Publishers, Inc., Wheaton, Illinois 60189.

Scripture quotations marked NIV are taken from the Holy Bible, NEW INTERNATIONAL VERSION®. Copyright © 1973, 1978, 1984 International Bible Society. All rights reserved throughout the world. Used by permission of International Bible Society.

Scripture quotations marked MSG are taken from THE MESSAGE. Copyright © 1993, 1994, 1995, 1996, 2000, 2001, 2002. Used by permission of NavPress Publishing Group.

Scripture quotations marked NASB are taken from the NEW AMERICAN STANDARD BIBLE®, Copyright © 1960, 1962, 1963, 1968, 1971, 1972, 1973, 1975, 1977, 1995 by The Lockman Foundation. Used by permission.

Laura-Lee Booth—Chief Editor

Library of Congress PCN: 2009907486

ISBN-13: 978-0-9825289-0-7

To the love of my life, Dr. Randy Valimont, who made me a minister's wife.

Acknowledgments

. . . .

Thank you, first of all, to my husband, Randy, who has encouraged, prodded, forced, and enabled me to complete this book.

To my daughters, Jordan, Danielle, and Alayna who have brought such joy to my life and provided me with untold examples of ministry, parenting, and a loving lifestyle.

To my parents, Rev. and Mrs. Gerald Jordan, who introduced me to Jesus and the ministry. Thank you for always living your lives above reproach.

To the pastoral staff and families at Griffin First Assembly of God, both past and present, who have prayed for me and added depth and richness to my life.

Table of Contents

SECTION III: *They Have Issues*

SECTION IV: *Time to Step Out*

Introduction

I can remember growing up in a minister's home and begging God to never make me be a preacher's wife. I knew my mother and I were not cut from the same cloth. Mom was the consummate lady and pastor's wife—always gracious in public, saying the right things, doing the right things, and she even looked like the "perfect preacher's wife" to the extent of never wearing makeup or pants. She did her best to make sure daddy was happy, and she never, ever complained. I can remember watching my mother sit on the front row every Sunday as the "soft support" for my dad. Not wanting to be an embarrassment or be considered "out of line" by our constituents, she never said a word out loud—not even an "amen." On many occasions, she would be moved to tears by a sermon illustration or a special song; but never to be unprepared, she would reach for the appropriate Kleenex® tucked away in her bag to gently dab away any tell-tale signs of her emotion of the moment. When financial times were tough in our home, mom had a very unique way of making us believe that hand-me-down clothes were so special, they just had to be worn again. She made everyone feel like royalty.

No one was ever a stranger at our house—not even unexpected company. Mom had that special knack of preparing just the right amount of food and made sure the extra person (or two or three) never left hungry. We often hosted visiting ministers in our home, which meant mom had to prepare our house for their visit and cook even more food. She accomplished all of these tasks in addition to keeping our household running smoothly and getting ready for church services, which she never missed any. Visiting ministers usually meant I had to abandon my bedroom and make adjustments. But Mama seemed to do all of this—and much, much more—in her high heels and Sunday best with a gentle smile on her face. And again, never with a complaint!

I could never understand how Mama's breath could always be so fresh. It always smelled like Listerine® during the day and wintergreen during church services. It didn't dawn on me until I was quite a bit older that she kept a small bottle of Listerine® in the kitchen for emergency mouthwash and a roll of those nasty Certs® in her handbag for church. Whenever I would spy her pop a Certs® in her mouth toward the end of service, I would quickly ask for one; to which she would reply, "This is not just candy; it's a breath freshener." (I have since tried that same tactic on my own kids, but they just don't buy the idea that chocolate is a genuine breath freshener.)

There were three of us girls, and I guess I was destined to be the black sheep—or so I would like to have thought. My older sister was too perfect to ever do anything wrong. She looked and acted like my mother, and I knew she was the ideal candidate for another "perfect pastor's wife." On the other hand, my baby sister was born ten years after me and was always too cute in her misdeeds to be interpreted as B-A-D. As for me, I tried everything I could to become deserving of the infamous "black sheep" title, but I was always afraid Mama or Daddy would catch me. To help their cause, there was always some old biddy who was up in my business and found great pleasure in making my private life known to the whole world—or so it seemed. I figured since two-out-of-three kids were good, Mama had to be happy. Surely, God would just give up on me and let my two sisters wear the badge she wore so admirably and dive headlong into the ministry. At that time, I never could imagine the rude awakening God had in store for me.

From the Pit to the Parsonage

When I was a teenager, my perfect mother felt that God called her to teach our teen Sunday School class. All of my peers thought she was the greatest, especially when she brought chocolate oatmeal cookies. She never complained about taking on another role in the church. In fact, she seemed to revel in it. (I secretly knew I could never teach teenagers; and after substituting one Sunday in the junior boys' class, I was quite sure even Jesus was afraid of them!) Not only did she teach, but she sang in the choir and stayed in the nursery when necessary. It was amazing to see. The more Mama worked, the more she blossomed. For me, I didn't mind singing, but that nursery duty stuff was off limits. I never thought babies smelled good—until I had my own.

After graduating from high school, I still knew that being a minister's wife was definitely not my calling. Instead, I enrolled in school to become a teacher, and figured I would win the world one student at a time. It seemed to be working just fine. We would pray in my class, and revival would change the whole school system where I would teach. A few years later, I ended up in a college I labeled as the P.I.T., which stood for "Preachers in Training." Holding firm to my self-induced calling made me avoid all the P.I.T.'s. like the plague! With confidence, I would shout it from the housetops, "I will never be a pastor's wife!" As soon as I announced that little tidbit of information, they all avoided me, as well. I did not fit the "perfect pastor's wife" prerequisites: one must play the piano, sing alto, wear the Pastor's Wife suit on Sunday mornings, and be ready to live in the proverbial glass bowl.

All of this seemed to be going very well except for one, small issue: no one ever told me that you never say, "Never,"—especially to God. Little did I know the whole time I was saying "Never," God was preparing my future husband to help me understand my reasons for not wanting to be in the ministry. I had a simple fear that I wouldn't measure up to MY own idea of what the "perfect pastor's wife" should be. I felt I would not, and could not, be as good as Mama.

Everything was clicking along according to plan—my plan, that is—until along came Randy. And, wouldn't you know it, I fell head-over-heels in love with a man who was destined to be a minister of the Gospel of Jesus Christ! His passion for God and his unmatched faith in God was contagious. At that point in time, I did not know these were the exact things I would need in my helpmate. My future husband was not only destined to be my life-partner, but the one God would use to help complete the work He had already started in me.

The funny thing was Mama already knew that I was not an image of her, and I would need a husband designed especially by God for me. My perfect, uncomplaining mother watched me walk down the aisle to not only join myself in marriage to the man I loved, but also join myself to a ministry and a future pastor. I'm sure I heard her laugh as I passed down the aisle. My "never" had just turned into my "I do," and God was about to take me on the ride of my life—a ride that I am still living to this day!

The Dreaded Seven-Letter Word

One of the main reasons I never wanted to be in the ministry was the misconception that I would have to be without blemish or, better yet, the dreaded seven-letter word: *perfect* (more on this subject in chapter one!) You see, I never took a college course or attended any workshops on how to be a minister's wife. No books were recommended to me, and there was not a "Pastor's Wives for Dummies" laying around at my local bookstore. When my husband applied for his credentials, no

one ever asked or even seemed to care about my qualifications, my education, my theology, or my belief system about the ministry. Nevertheless,
there I was in this vast area of the unknown world of ministry. Although
being raised in a pastor's home somewhat prepared me for the expectations of this journey, nothing could have adequately prepared me for the
real experience. But, I wasn't alone. I quickly found that many women
who followed God and their husband into the ministry did so with no
real idea of what to expect.

Lord knows there was never a shortage of well-meaning women
who were ready to tell me their own version of the "perfect pastor's
wife." Unfortunately, most of these women had never been in the
ministry. Rather, they had compiled a list throughout the years of what
they wanted in their "perfect pastor's wife." Their description was a
usually a hybrid of the power of Kathryn Kuhlman, the graciousness
of Jackie Kennedy-Onassis, the domestication of Martha Stewart, the
love for the poor of Mother Theresa's, and the teaching ability of Joyce
Meyer. There's one thing they forgot, though. That person doesn't really
exist. She's a figment of their imagination—*and they forgot to tell me!*

I always hated the Proverbs 31 woman because even her children
thought she was perfect! Now, my kids think a lot of things about me,
but perfection is not one them. What I have to come to realize is this:
Solomon, the writer of Proverbs, condensed her life down to a mere 21
verses which beautifully describe all of the virtues she possesses. But,
he did not say she was all of these things on the same day! They were
lifetime achievements. For example, the passage that says, *"Her children
rise up and call her blessed,"*[1] probably did not apply when they were being
disciplined for throwing a temper tantrum in the grocery store or being
grounded for the rest of their lives after doing exactly what she had told

---

1 Proverbs 31:28 (NKJV)

them not to. These were grown up children, possibly with spouses and families of their own to care for. Wow, I guess this means there's hope for me! I can have all of those virtues—*one at a time*. I can rise up early and go about my duties, but not when I've been up all night with a sick baby. I can be vigorous, but not after I've just prepared enough food for an army. I can do all of those things, occasionally . . . but not all day, every day, or even right now. Sometimes.

Don't get me wrong, there is no sin in striving to be the best you can be without regard to your life's vocation. In fact, God's Word tells us to try our best to be our best. But, often we forget about the end of Proverbs 31 which says, "A woman who fears the Lord, she shall be praised."[2] At the end of the day, it won't be about all the things we have done, the ministries we have created or maintained, or the "perfection" we have tried to achieve; but it will come down to the wisdom, understanding, and the fear of the Lord we have obtained and walked in. All the things on the outside truly do fade.

Issues = Is Shoes

*W*hen I set out to write this book, I knew there were several items—better known as issues—which needed to be covered. So, I thought, "Hey, why not tie these subjects into something every woman can obviously relate to?" And that, my friend, is shoes! Don't laugh; you know it's true. I love them, you love them, we all love them! It doesn't matter what race, ethnic background, social status, or career choice; we love shoes! And, whether we want to admit it or not, our lives mystically revolve around the selection of footwear which inhabits our closets. The right pair of shoes can make a bad day turn around and

---

2 Proverbs 31:30b

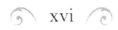

completely change our outlook on life.

In the following pages, you will find chapters like "The Issue Box," "Footings," "Bronzed Shoes," and "House Shoes"—all dealing with very specific issues we, as minister's wives, face.

The title may be funny, but there are some very special messages I want you to know while reading about the "shoes" of life. Things like:

* You can win.

* You can be successful.

* You can be all God designed you to be.

If you strive to be anything at all, be authentic at the highest level. Authenticity is the beginning of success. Sure, you will have faults and inadequacies, but who doesn't?

There are a few things I've learned these past few years in ministry. I'm definitely not the "expert," but I believe the following pages will encourage, inspire, and most of all enlighten the areas where women in ministry so often struggle. The most important thing I can share with you is to follow God with all of your heart and to just be yourself. God only needed one of my mother; and hopefully, He made only one of me!

Are you ready? Let's walk together!

Footnote:

"Shoes are my kind of therapy."

The Issue Box

My Issue: *Perfection*

*W*henever I buy a new pair of shoes, I immediately take them out of the box and put them in a shoe file according to how they will fit into my life. It's quite simple: black shoes go together, followed by brown. Then off-white, white, red, navy, yellow, gold, silver, and multi-colored ones are next. Slides go together as well as pumps. Both sandals and boots have a place of their own, and tennis shoes go way in the back because I hardly ever need them. Bedroom slippers can be placed in the same file because they crush or fold so easily. Even though this systematic way to organize one of the most important facets of the female life is a bit compulsive, it pales in comparison to other situations I have encountered.

Take, for instance, my cousin, Shirley. Like me, she is married to a minister. He told me he had to add an entire room to their house just for Shirley's shoe collection. But guess what? It still was not enough room, so she did the next, most logical thing—she took over *his* closet! I'm not saying my problem is a case of family genetics, but it is definitely one of gender genetics. Face it—every woman loves shoes! I have never met a woman yet who did not share this same infatuation. It's in our blood!

Just as I have never met a woman who didn't like shoes, I have never met a woman who didn't have issues—and plenty of them. For me, the problem is I cannot methodically store them in a box or a file, because they would eventually keep cropping up. Some in unexpected places. Even if I built a special room like Shirley's husband did, it still wouldn't be enough space. Whether I like it or not, the biggest issue with my issues is that I cannot hide them away forever. I must face them and deal with them.

Just What is "Perfect" Anyway?

I have searched for years to find the perfect pair of shoes and have recently come to a shocking conclusion: perfect shoes do not exist! There are many great shoes, some even serve a particular purpose, some that almost match, and some that are, oh, so close to perfection—but no perfect ones. When my husband asked me, "Honey, is there such a thing as the perfect pair of shoes?" I find myself breaking out the old hymn, "No not one, no not one," much to his dismay.

Styles change, people change, demands change, and even feet will change. The pair of shoes that were "just fine" last year may not work the very next year for the exact same task. But, you never throw them out, because they might work the following year. It's funny how that works, but it's true nonetheless! Over the years, instead of being on the constant quest for the perfect pair, I've come to realize that when I relax in the shoes I need for a particular day, whether pumps or sandals, I am well-equipped for that day.

In the same way, the quest for perfection haunted me as a new minister's wife. I often wished I knew exactly what it was I was supposed to do and exactly how I was supposed to look. Finding just about anything and everything under the sun online was a cinch, but there was no website advertising the latest "perfect pastor's wife" handbook. And believe me, I looked!

Randy and I began our ministry journey as youth pastors, and immediately I was awakened to the real world of well-meaning people trying to help me be the perfect wife. So many times I would hear, "You don't even look like a pastor's wife!" and I would be afraid I had really messed up—even if I was just wearing loungewear or blue jeans. One lady in a department store told me that only "loose" women (in today's vernacular, "hoochie girls") wear shorts. She quickly told me, "We don't expect to see our pastor's wife dressed like that at K-mart®." Unfortunately for this dear saint of God, she said the wrong thing on the wrong day. I was hot, tired, and moving into a city where we knew no one. I was frustrated, had a crying baby, and I couldn't find my screwdriver to put up my mini-blinds. I was quick to speak my mind, letting her know that I was not yet on staff and thus not available for her criticism. Fortunately for me, she apologized and became the epitome of graciousness personified.

These moments of epiphany brought me to the reality that there was a certain "look" for minister's wives. Unfortunately, of all the ones I had ever met, none were my age, and I really questioned if they ever had been! They were all much older than me—more like a mother figure—and all carried the same longsuffering expression like they had just spent the last 50 years on a remote continent where being stylish was equated to ungodliness. My desire was to be a Godly woman, but I also wanted to look as good as possible and not be offensive in my attire or my attitude. So began my quest for how the "perfect pastor's wife" should look.

I figured since nurses and doctors, police officers, and firemen have their uniforms; maintenance people have uniforms, some school children get uniforms, and even the Pope has a uniform, it would be easy to find a minister's wife uniform. Right? Wrong. I have still yet to find a shop which advertises: "We have uniforms for the perfect pastor's wife!" There are advertisements for short women, tall women, plus-sized women, brides, babies, the college-bound student, ethnic celebrations, climates, and every other style that you can possibly imagine, but nothing for the pastor's wife. I searched and searched but always came up empty-handed, which only added to my frustration.

After a while of searching, I began to think, "What if you actually *could* go online and order up the 'perfect pastor's wife'? That would solve all the issues." But then, the thought occurred to me that this "perfect wife" might come from a company like Mattel®, Smart Pets®, or Robotics Incorporated®, which would make for another whole set of problems.

Can you imagine the Barbie® pastor's wife? She would come equipped with a rock-hard figure complete with a tiny waistline. She would only wear stiletto heels all day, and she would always have a smile—even if it was just a plastic one—on her worst day. And to boot, she's married to Pastor "Ken" who is also perfect in every way and completely idolizes her.

The Smart Pets® pastor's wife is well-trained enough to go into the store without making a mess. She never begs for treats (a.k.a. "attention"), never holds a grudge against her master (the pastor, of course), and her only desire is to fetch and carry (a.k.a. "to serve"). If she's good enough on a certain task, she can expect the well-deserved "treat" and a pat on the head (words of affirmation from the deacon board and their wives).

How about the Robotics pastor's wife? She only does what she is programmed to do and does it well, with expertise. She never makes a mistake, and if she does, it's because of a human error incorrect data input (a.k.a. "miscommunication"). She never has to eat, sleep, or even rest, and she's always available in an instant. She does not know the word "no" because it has never been programmed into her hard drive.

Wouldn't one of these be great? The only problem was, I was none of them and, honestly, did not have any desire to become something from a box. Come to think of it, I've never quite fit into the proverbial "minister's family" box!

The Perception of Perfection

*A*s a teenager, I never wanted to fit the mold of the typical pastor's kid—better known as a "PK." Now, some years later, I'm finding the same desire to not fit the mold of the typical pastor's wife—whatever that might be. I have discovered the only mold that ever existed was self-made in the minds of those who have never lived, served, or held any position of ministry. Their misconceptions of how the pastor's wife should look, what she should do, and her decorum is so confusing; no one could ever match the criteria. For example, the pre-molded pastor's wife should:

* Look good . . . but not too good. "You can't be the prettiest woman in the church!"

* Have nice clothes . . . but not nicer than the other women in leadership.

* Have a current style to your hair . . . but not a trendy look. Good color but only subtle highlights—nothing brassy or ostentatious which could draw attention to yourself.

* Possess good teeth to smile a lot when the pastor is being somewhat funny . . . but be able to frown and show disgust expressively when he speaks of sin.

* Only wear make-up to enhance what God gave you and never to cover up any imagined flaws—for we are, after all, "perfect."

* Speak to young girls but never, ever, under any circumstances mention the "S" word—you know . . . SEX—because ministers and their wives are far above that! (Why, even their children are conceived through immaculate conception!)

* Keep our homes spotless, uncluttered, swept, and mopped every day.

* Always have enough food prepared to feed those who stop by unexpected.

And if those were not enough, then came the requirements for our families:

* Your children can never misbehave. They must always sit neatly dressed on the front pew and listen closely to the

sermon—regardless of their ages.

* The pastor's wife should always make sure the pastor looks handsome, is clean-shaven, shirt freshly pressed, and shoes shined to the finest.

After all, we *are* the perfect family in the perfect church with the perfect life. Right? This would be so nice. If only it was true. But in reality, it's only a perception and is far from actuality. Just as perception is not reality, neither is perfection. Perception is only real to the person who perceives it. What is perfect for one person may not be the standard of perfection for another. What people perceive to be perfect is perfect only to them.

What people perceive to be perfect is perfect only to them.

When I was in high school, I wanted to be just like Katy. I thought she was absolutely beautiful with her blonde hair, blue eyes, long legs, and her early developments (if you know what I mean). Katy always had a lot of friends, and she certainly never went a week without a boyfriend. Katy's dad did not live with them, but she never seemed to care or miss him. She and her mom were best friends, shopping together, eating together, even partying together. Based on what I saw,

I perceived Katy would succeed in anything she did just because of her beauty and countless friends and relationships. I never knew Katy was on an endless search for happiness, trying to fill an empty void through surface friendships. Her relentless stream of boyfriends was her way of obtaining male attention and approval which she desperately missed and needed from her absentee father.

Fifteen years after high school, I saw Katy again. It was only then I came to realize my perception was far from the truth as her beauty, friends, relationships with boys, and partying had led to her premature aging and chronic cynicism with mankind in general. My *perception* of her life was not her *reality*. I, then, realized what Katy needed all along was a friend who could tell her the truth and lead her to a relationship with Jesus. That friend could have been me. Instead, she only got someone who was full of envy toward her.

Perception is usually far from reality.

Will the Real You Please Stand Up?

Why do we always desire to be someone we are not? Why do we strive to look like someone else? Television programs show us exactly what we need to do to look like a particular star. Extreme makeovers can radically change our hairstyle, make-up, and even give us pre-worn clothing once belonging to a famous star, just to make that dream come true. Remember, that star doesn't always look "perfect" in everyday life. The next time you are checking out of the grocery store, just look at some of the pictures which end up in the tabloids! Countless hours in the beauty shop, glued on eyelashes, implants, liposuction, Botox, and the miracle of computer technology and airbrushed photography can make just about anyone look like a star, but it's not reality. Why do you think there are body doubles used in movies? It's simple. If the star's behind doesn't suit the producer, it's okay to just get a "behind double" that's a little firmer and easier on the eyes. Again, this is not reality.

Just think what I might be able to look like every Sunday morning if I had someone else get me ready to meet my adoring public (a.k.a congregation)? Hair done, make-up perfect, clothes tailored, nails manicured—aah, there she is . . . the "perfect pastor's wife." Well, there's only one problem with this scenario: it's just not me! And truthfully, instead of spending hours letting someone else get me ready, I would much rather spend hours myself getting people ready to meet Jesus! Now *that's* reality.

Another reality is that no one has been called to be a Barbie®, Smart Pets®, or "robot" pastor's wife. All that is required of you is to be the woman God has called you to be—period. In searching for authenticity and determining who that person is and how she should appear, here are a couple of things to keep before you:

1. **Answer this question before you try to help anyone else find themselves.** "Who am I in Christ, and what is He requiring of me?" Come to an understanding that God truly loves and cares for you *just as you are.* He only needs one of you, not a carbon copy of the former pastor's wife, or what someone else thinks you should be. First and foremost, be pleasing to God—not the church, the church board, or the women's ministry leaders.

2. **Don't allow people to interpret your freedom.** Don't become bound by what people think as uncaring of the role you represent. You are the minister's wife, and you do have a role to fill. You can be the greatest asset your husband has in

the ministry, or you can be the greatest burden. If you truly don't care, this will be evident in other areas of your life.

As much as we would like to deny it, we are examples in leadership, and some people would like to use us as a mirror of themselves. If we are to be a true reflection, let it be of the attitude of Jesus Christ and of servanthood, not a reflection of free thinking. The prophet, Isaiah, described the Daughters of Zion in the prophecy concerning the Day of the Lord. It was haughty thinking that destroyed them, and we need to be cautious not to embrace this type of worldly attitudes.

> *"Moreover, the Lord said, 'Because the daughters of Zion are proud, and walk with heads held high and seductive eyes, and go along with mincing steps and tinkle the bangles on their feet, therefore the Lord will afflict the scalp of the daughters of Zion with scabs, and the Lord will make their foreheads bare.' In that day, the Lord will take away the beauty of their anklets, headbands, crescent ornaments, dangling earrings, bracelets, veils, headdresses, ankle chains, sashes, perfume boxes, amulets, finger rings, nose rings, festal robes, outer tunics, cloaks, money purses, hand mirrors, undergarments, turbans, and veils. Now it will come about that instead of sweet perfume there will be putrefaction; instead of a belt, a rope; instead of well-set hair, a plucked-out scalp; instead of fine clothes, a donning of sackcloth; and branding instead of beauty.'"*

ISAIAH 3:16-24

3. **Stay current.** In all aspects of life, including your clothing styles, but more importantly in your way of thinking. You should strive to be stylish, but sometimes classic styles work the best because current styles change so frequently and with every season. Don't spend a lot of money on trendy clothing. Instead, look for something very versatile that can be worn for many occasions. Believe it or not, thrift stores and garage sales are a great place to find the "deal of the century." Trendy doesn't necessarily mean expensive, especially if it is an accessory which can compliment something you already have hanging in your closet.

    While staying stylish in all manners of dress, remain modest. Remember, not only are all the *women* in the church watching what you wear every Sunday, the *men* are watching you, as well! You can be in style without being an exhibitionist. Low-cut tops, pants that are too tight, slacks or skirts that expose your mid-drift or underwear have no place in the attire of the Godly woman and certainly not in the wardrobe of a minister's wife. To purposely wear clothing that is blatantly immodest is to stir up lust in the heart of a man, which opens the door to sin.

4. **Take care of your physical body.** Women today have a way of thinking we are totally invincible, pushing ourselves until there is nothing left. It's no wonder we fall into bed at night with our husbands and are left asking each other, "Where has all the romance gone?" As you read this, I give you the freedom to not be Wonder Woman® or a superwoman and to be "only one woman."

    There are many roles we all must fill: daughter,

wife, mom, nurse, domestic engineer, money manager, business administrator, counselor, nurse, companion, friend, confidante, and the list goes on and on, just like the Energizer Bunny™. Too bad those commercials never tell us that the batteries eventually *do* run down and have to be re-charged or thrown out. You never want your batteries to run down so that YOU have to be replaced! The first way to take care of your physical body is to look at your duties and ask yourself a few important questions like:

* Can I give up some activity?

* Am I busy just to be busy?

* Am I over-involved?

* Have I taken on a duty just because I could do it better than anyone else?

* Am I sacrificing my time at the cost of my health?

These questions, answered honestly, can begin alleviating some of the overworked areas of your life you may be experiencing.

In early 1984, Randy and I began our first senior pastorate. As with most new pastors and their families, we made many mistakes, mainly because we were ignorant and too young to know any better. One of the huge mistakes I made was saying, "Yes" to everything and everybody, not ever realizing I was allowed to say, "No." In the midst of all this, we added another baby to our own family along with adding baby Christians to the family of God. We all know both of those are very time consuming. Days and nights, including weekends, were being filled counseling and disciplining these young Christians. I had a breastfeeding baby, a strong-willed toddler, and a husband who had to counsel on the phone during dinner. We had no time to truly call our own. Many times someone would stop by to just ask Randy a quick question, but those "quick questions" would often turn into dessert and coffee, a Bible Study, or a lengthy debate. There were times I even came out in my pajamas as a hint to end the discussion and come to bed, but all I got were compliments on how cute I was. I threatened Randy that if these late nights didn't stop, next time I would come out in a negligee! But, our nights kept getting later, and mornings came earlier.

As the church grew, I became the pre-school director, music minister, high school girls' leader, sectional director for the women's ministries for our area, the food pantry coordinator, and the funeral meals team leader. All of this was "volunteer work" which basically meant there was no pay. In the meanwhile, we started our children in school. We began building a church only to watch a tornado blow it down. So, we re-started and finished building a new church with a boys' outreach building, hired and fired staff, built our own house, moved our family across town, entertained 21 of the first 23 days in our new home, and continued to add to my list of jobs. All of this without getting any smarter.

After one particularly trying day, I found myself crying in my office, unable to stop. I left work and went home to prepare dinner, but the tears would not stop. Finally, pulling myself together, I decided to go buy groceries. Then my crying turned into anger. I was mad at Randy, mad at my kids, mad at the church, and mad at God for making me do all of this work . . . or so it seemed. Pulling into our driveway with the car full of groceries, I began to think that I really didn't have to continue dealing with this pressure. All I had to do was just let go. And I started to do just that. I don't know how long I sat there, but Randy came and found me staring off into empty space, unable to respond. I had begun the process of truly letting go, but only letting go of my own mind. There is no doubt I came within moments of a complete nervous breakdown.

Randy called both our parents and everyone began to pray. God brought me back to reality; however, I knew this experience was a true wake-up call from the Holy Spirit. It was time to pull back from my activities, learn to relax, and say, "No!" or suffer the consequences in my mind and body. Through God's grace, I learned that His yoke really is easy and His burden is light (see Matthew 11:30). The burden I found myself carrying did not belong to God; it was self-induced and was anything but light.

5. **Assess your day off.** Do you really take some time to recoup your strength? Do you feed your spirit and your soul with rest? Do you fall into the trap of Satan which says, "If I don't do it, nobody else will?" You may be right. Maybe no one else will, but it's okay to leave dirty dishes in the sink while you take a bubble bath! One of the problems with not taking time to recoup is that it produces a very high sense of frustration when you cannot accomplish

tasks because fatigue will not allow you to.

6. **Do your exercise.** First Timothy 4:7 says, *". . . On the other hand, discipline yourself for the purpose of godliness."* The Proverbs 31 woman even "girds herself with strength."[1] (Another reason why I really don't like that woman very much.) Exercising is really not my idea of a fun time. I do not like to increase my heart rate. I do not like to sweat. I do not like to run. I do not like sports or all that it entails; but I do like to feel well, feel good about myself, and have some stamina. So, I will do my exercises. One thing you will learn is this: when you discipline yourself enough to exercise, it will help to bring discipline into other areas of your life.

When you discipline yourself enough to exercise, it will help to bring discipline into other areas of your life.

7. **Find a mentor, a coach, or a hero.** This is someone you can look up to, preferably someone who has been where you are walking. It will help you to keep things in perspective and give you strength, knowing someone else has been where you are *and* survived to tell about it. God has gifted my life with

---

1 Proverbs 31:17

so many women—many whom I know personally and some of whom I just admire the way they live for Jesus. Among my peers and mentors, there are women who have become gifts of encouragement, gifts of music, gifts of character and stamina, and gifts of authenticity. Along with your mentor, find a ministry woman with whom you can become friends. You might find your friendship, and the help and encouragement it brings, can be mutually beneficial.

So, who is this woman, the pastor's wife: a career woman, a preacher in her own right, a mom, a barren woman, or a woman with lots of children? Is she skinny, plump, tall, short, blonde, brunette, loud, quiet, musical, tone-deaf, creative, disorganized, stylish, black, white, red, or brown? Does she like short dresses, long dresses, or just slacks? Does she always wear high heels, or does she prefer flat shoes? She may be all of those things; and yet, the most important of all, is that she is truly a child of the Most High King. She is a princess—not perfect—with a closet full of shoes . . . and a life full of issues.

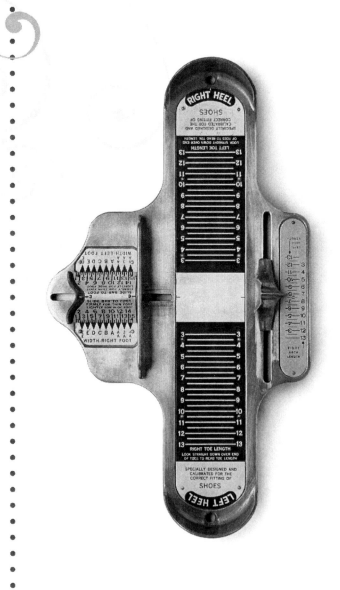

Footnote:

"Peace on earth, cute shoes to all."

2

That Measuring Thingy

MY ISSUE: *MEASURING UP*

I once worked in the shoe department at a local department store—talk about heaven on earth! And even though I could tell you every shoe brand, shape, and size in stock, I could never remember the proper name of the measuring device we had to use. You know, that gray metal, sliding apparatus which tells you the length and width you need? I just always referred to it as "that measuring thingy." It made a great toy for little kids who came in with their moms and siblings. Most of the time, I would just put them to work measuring each other's feet, which provided great entertainment and made my job easier at the same time. It also made for a pretty handy, make-shift paddle for more than one harried mom to use on her young 'uns. But, that's for another story!

This type of equipment was not around when I was a child, so my parents had a really innovative idea when it came to measuring us girls for new shoes. It all began in the days when laundry detergent was packaged in cardboard boxes. In our house, an empty box *never* went to waste and was always used for something—a garbage box, a paint canvas, or a snow sled. (I guess you could say we were into recycling before it was posh to be "green.") When it came time for new shoes, daddy would reach into his front pants pocket, pull out his big knife, and turn the detergent box into a flat piece of cardboard. He would call me over to stand on the cardboard and say, "Now, stand up straight." Once I was standing as straight as possible, he would trace a line around my foot—much like drawing around your hands and decorating your fingers with rings. Trimming the cardboard around the edges produced the "foot line," and we would either take it to the shoe store or send it to my cousin who sold shoes in Nashville. If the cardboard foot line fit in the shoe, the store would mail the correct pair to our home. This process was great for my dad as he did not have to listen to me deciding on the "perfect" pair! Actually, he chose the size (which, of course, was always one size larger for room to grow) and decided the style and the color. It was always brown, black, or white. In those days, colorful shoes were only for the rich.

This system worked great until dad stopped getting accurate measurements of my foot, mostly due to me being so antsy and unable to stand still for a whopping five minutes. He was convinced that whatever outline he sent was correct. Most of the time, we were running around at the last moment—Saturday night before Sunday service—so if my shoe didn't fit, I was faced with two options: wear the new, uncomfortable shoe or wear the old, uncomfortable pair one more time. Which would you choose? My point, exactly! Actually, all of this drama would have been avoided if the measurements had been right in the beginning.

should be at a certain level too quickly. Unlike other job descriptions, there is no true evaluation form. However, there are some great things from the Bible to take into consideration when assessing yourself:

1. **You will be weighed in the balance.** According to the prophet, Daniel, God will do the weighing. Don't be found wanting or lacking by God (see Daniel 5:27).

2. **You will go through many changes in the course of your life.** The balance of God will be just and equitable for each particular season. If you are young, you may be raising babies, and your priorities should reflect those of raising Godly children. As you mature and the seasons of your life change, so will your priorities. Changing your focus in life or ministry is totally normal and does not make you more or less spiritual. Much like fruit that matures over seasons, your character and spiritual life develops over time.

3. **Find your strength and focus on it.** Remember your strengths and weaknesses both change. There will be times when you will be more energetic than others. During one season you may find yourself teaching small children but, at another, feel God leading you to teach adults. You may feel the desire to sing in the choir for a season; and in another, move away from the music ministry department entirely. I have found in my own life that when God calls me to do something, it is not because I can, but because He wants me to find a new strength and develop it.

· ·

When God calls me to do something, it is not because I can, but because He wants me to find a new strength and develop it.

· ·

4. **Don't compare your weakness to someone else's strength.** You will always lose. Period.

> *"Then Saul gave David his own armor—a bronze helmet and a coat of mail. David put it on, strapped the sword over it, and took a step or two to see what it was like, for he had never worn such things before. 'I can't go in these,' he protested. 'I'm not used to them.' So he took them off again."*
>
> **1 SAMUEL 17:38-39 (NLT)**

When David went to battle against Goliath, Saul wanted David to wear his armor, but there was only one problem—it was way too large for him. It was armor custom designed for the King of Israel, not a shepherd boy. The helmet slipped down over his face, and he could not see. The sword was too heavy for him to carry. The garment was too long, and David had not found the time to test Saul's armor. Saul thought he was doing David a favor because it had worked for him; but if David had gone into battle with the wrong armor, it could have been his death. He would have been depending on man and not on the name of LORD.

Don't be like David, going into battle for the Kingdom trying to be someone you are not and wearing another man's armor. You haven't tested it, you cannot see clearly, and the burden of the sword is too heavy. You will trip on the garment which is too long and end up with your backside exposed to the enemy. Failure is inevitable when you enter in battle in your own strength or in someone else's armor.

5. **Perception is not reality.** I know we covered this topic in the first chapter, but it needs to be reiterated due to its nature and seriousness. It is one of the major culprits that derails so many minister's wives, and it does not need to go unnoticed. Perception may seem real, look real, and even feel real; but in reality, it may be only an illusion. Here are a few examples of perception versus reality that many wives in the ministry constantly face:

PERCEPTION: You have a charmed life. You never seem to have any problems.
REALITY: If you could only see the curse I am fighting now—and it is not charming!

PERCEPTION: Your children are so well-behaved and never make any messes.
REALITY: Go look under their beds, in their backpacks, and in their cars!

PERCEPTION: Your husband is so Godly. It must be like heaven living with him.

REALITY: Sometimes it does seem like an eternity, although not in heaven!

6. **Be authentic at the highest level.** If you are a true steward of Christ, you have no choice but to be authentic. To put on a façade or to try to be something you are not is to deny everything Christ teaches about servanthood. Be yourself and be faithful to the end.

> *"Let a man regard us in this manner, as servants of Christ and stewards of the mysteries of God."*

> 1 CORINTHIANS 4:1

Regardless of what place you are in life, find those things God is requiring of you. Different life experiences will enable you to minister from what you have learned and gleaned from. Your past failures and heartaches, current joys and sorrows, and dreams for the future are all built around who you are and how God chooses to use you. According to Philippians 1:6, God is beginning a new work in you, and He is always faithful to complete it. He will never leave you hanging!

So, live up to where you are and let God use whatever He desires in your life. Come to peace with who you are. Develop your own personal security and identity based on the fact that your value is not based upon your love for God, but rather, His love for you!

And by the way, throw away that measuring thingy!

Footnote:

"Life is short—buy the shoes."

3

The Power of the Sole

My Issue: *Planning Ahead*

The type of work you do will determine the type of shoes you wear. For instance, if you are a roofer, you will need different shoes than a dancer. The well-equipped, rugged construction worker will probably wear a very sturdy, steel-toed shoe or boots with the sole suitably reinforced. This is to keep the foot from being injured. Tennis shoes just don't work on construction sites. My husband found this out the hard way.

While living in Toccoa, Georgia, a tornado ripped through our city, destroying one of our church buildings. Church members and pastoral staff alike worked tirelessly in the clean-up efforts. Many of these people knew what to expect and thus came equipped with the proper gloves, hard hats, and the right shoes. But Randy, along with a few more, only came with what they were wearing at the time.

Although steel-toed boots should be a necessity for any minister's wardrobe, for some reason Randy had left them off his "well-equipped pastor" list! Instead, he showed up promptly at the work site ready to dive in and help with the sturdiest shoes he owned—*canvas tennis shoes*. It wasn't long before he stepped on a rusty nail which penetrated all the way through the massive, quarter-inch sole of his shoe and straight into his foot. In essence, his tennis shoe was now nailed to his foot! It was not a pretty sight. He did not cry— even though he probably wanted to—and I did not laugh—even though I wanted to! (Good for both of us.) Of course, this promptly changed his location from the clean-up site to the emergency room, where the dreaded tetanus shot was waiting for him!

Had his sole been properly equipped for the job, the nail would have never gotten through the first layer. As it was, Randy's tennis shoe was only equipped to handle daily wear and tear or the basketball court, at best. Even though he had not planned to use these particular shoes for such a task, it became necessary. The lesson learned was the power of the sole was only strong enough for its intended use—and now, he had the bruise and shot in the arm to prove it!

Life is much like this scenario. We need the right footwear to travel through construction and building zones. Steel-toed boots and steel-reinforced soles help us maneuver through areas filled with debris. If you come wearing tennis shoes, you just might get a nail through your foot.

Proper planning is a major key to success in ministry or any other facet of life.

Life Beyond Sunday Morning

Living a life in the ministry can make you feel as if you are just living day-to-day—not planning for the future or expecting to see good things happen in your personal or professional life. Too often, we allow the events of the past or the apathy of the moment to blur our vision of reality. It's much like driving a car by only looking out the rear view mirror. We see road signs but can't read them. See cars but no occupants. See people but not their expressions. The elements of weather can be all around us, but we cannot see the sun, the rainbow, or the beauty of God's creation. Everything in life is passing us by, and the only opportunity to enjoy them is seemingly found in a revisit. Unfortunately, life has no remote control with a rewind or fast-forward button.

Have you ever spent so much time looking at what has already happened that you didn't make an effort to *make* things happen? Do you ever wonder if one day you will look back and wonder just what all of your time, energy, and effort has produced? Sure you have. We all have. At times, we all question if we are accomplishing what God has intended us to do. Did we have a goal, a dream, a vision? Or, did we just do what was expected at the time we were expected to do it?

Solomon tells us in Proverbs 29:18 (KJV):

"Where there is no vision, the people perish . . ."

I have watched so many minister's wives quote this scripture to their congregation, their leaders, and their peers, yet never apply it to their own lives. Their day-to-day routine has taken its toll on them and turned goals into daily chores and dreams in redundant activity. This is a sad scenario, but it is all too common with those who serve other people above themselves. In all of your serving, remember: *God has a plan for you!* He has a great future and a vision for the things yet to come! He has a specified plan for your children, your husband, and your ministry. Start seeing the big picture God has ordained for you. Dream again. Have a vision past next Sunday's service or next month's ladies meeting. Take some time and plan for what you believe God has placed in your heart. Maybe it's for next year or for the next five or 20 years down the road. The more you dream it and prepare for it, the more real it will become on the inside of you. As the old saying goes, "If you fail to plan, then you are planning to fail."

Really finding what God has in store for you for the long-haul can, at times, produce more frustration than comfort, especially if you don't even know where to start. Wherever you are in the process, take these few questions to heart. I believe they can provide your life with great direction and focus.

The Plan: WHAT DO YOU WANT TO DO?

*C*an you identify something tucked away in the recesses of your soul which is just waiting for a better time, the right time, or maybe a just a "someday"? Do you remember what you dreamed of doing while you were a child or a teenager? Better yet, where do you see yourself in two years, five years, or 20 years? Someone once said, "If you aim at nothing, you'll hit it every time." This is so true. So the question is: what are you aiming at? Don't be afraid to have a dream for all the different areas and phases of your life. But, you have to start by aiming at something.

I normally don't watch daytime television—mostly due to the amount of sensationalism and immorality found on so many programs. However, one day I happened to be surfing the channels and saw a program where a beautiful young lady was pursuing a divorce from her husband. The most intriguing thing to me was that her and husband were in the ministry. This lady had always wanted to be a pastor's wife—you know, the "First Lady" of the church—but her husband was not pursuing the ministry quickly enough for her liking. Once she realized her dream was much more than the glamour of Sunday mornings (which, by the way, I'm still looking for!), she was extremely disappointed and disheartened. The day-to-day ministry grind had taken its toll, and her fairy-tale destiny in life had miserably crumbled to ashes right in her own hands. Now, it was time to do the next, "rational" thing—leave her husband and family to move on to her next dream! It was obvious this lady was only pursuing a title rather than the call of God for her life.

The plans you make for your future must be those which have been inspired by God, not something you have conjured up yourself. You have to be able to discern between what is reality and façade. Rest assured, if God has inspired your dream, He will make it come to pass. It will be real, attainable, and produce the most satisfaction and fulfillment you could ever imagine.

The Projection: IS IT A SHORT-TERM OR A LONG-TERM GOAL?

The young lady I watched on television had only aimed for a short-term goal. She had not thought about what it would take to make it past the wedding ceremony or what it would take to get into real ministry. Her only goal was to look good in the eyes of all her parishioners on Sunday mornings. The fallacy was revealed once her short-term goal had been reached. There was no substance to keep her there or motivate her to move forward; thus, the decision to walk away from it all. She completely missed the opportunity to plan for the future and, in the mean time, better herself at what she had already attained. What she really needed was a plan or a design moving her toward a future goal for her life in ministry—not a divorce lawyer.

It does not matter if you are going to be a wife, mother, teacher, nurse, ditch digger, or seamstress. Just be better than you were yesterday and less than you will be tomorrow.

* * *

> *Just be better than you were yesterday and less than you will be tomorrow.*

* * *

The Purpose: WHY DO YOU WANT TO ACHIEVE THIS DREAM?

When you identify what it is you really want, the next step is to identify the reason—or the ultimate purpose—which will drive you to achieve it. There have been years of teaching and many wonderful books written about the importance of purpose, so I will not spend time repeating what has already been so adequately written. But, one thing I have learned over the years is this: *purpose drives vision and dreams.* Basically, if you cannot answer the question "why?" then you have no reason or motivation to complete your goal. Ask yourself these simple questions concerning your future dreams:

* What is the motive behind my dream?

* Is it for personal accolades and success only? Or, will it benefit the Kingdom of God while helping me, as well?

* Will it be a positive thing for my husband and for my family?

* Is this something I can leave for my children and grandchildren to enjoy or continue?

One of the most important factors in pursuing a dream is hearing the leading and direction of God. Have you heard God say, "Yes, this is the time?" Sometimes, God will make you wait on your dream; not to dangle the proverbial carrot in front of your nose, but rather, so He can burn the desire deeper and deeper into your heart. When your purpose and ultimate end desire is so deeply engrained in your spirit, nothing will dissuade you from going after it.

When your purpose and ultimate end desire is so deeply engrained in your spirit, nothing will dissuade you from going after it.

I Have Issues

The Pursuit: HOW WILL YOU ACHIEVE THIS DREAM?

I often tease my husband about being the "dreamer" of our family. Sometimes, I think his name should have been "Joseph." I am the detailed person, which is one of the many reasons God put us together! He dreams the dreams, and then it's my job to figure out how we will get there. It's not that he is incapable of making the dream come to pass. He is very capable. But most of his time is spent dreaming more dreams, which doesn't leave him much time to work out the logistics of the last three or four! As soon as I complete the detailed path of how we will do a certain thing, he says, "Great, now here's another one." To say the least, it definitely keeps us on our toes.

Now that you are dreaming again, here are a few things to help make them come to pass:

1. **Make a plan of action.** It's great to dream, but dreams must have an accompanying plan of action, or they will just die as fantasies. For example, just dreaming about finishing your education will not make you wake up one day to find a degree hanging on your wall. You have to make plans and take it one step at a time. For any dream to come to pass, there will be times you feel as though you are sprinting, sometimes walking, other times crawling, and still other times where you feel no forward progress whatsoever. Be encouraged! It's all part of the process! But do not lose sight of the goal you have set before you. Here is a life lesson I have learned (the hard way): if you never dream and never plan, then you will never do. Always have the end in your sight.

If you never dream and never plan, then you will never do.

2. **Begin when the time is right.** My desire as a young girl was to learn sign language. I thought it was a beautiful way to communicate, and I always loved using my hands for anything. Unfortunately, my college degree program did not allow any time for me to take the appropriate classes. Not to be denied, I tried to teach myself by buying books, watching videos, hiring a tutor, using workbooks, closely observing others, and asking questions but could never master the language. I felt as though I had done all I could do by adjusting my time and seeking outside training. Although I was not successful at this particular time, I never lost focus of the end desire and continued to ask God for His direction and steps. The timing was just not right.

It was not until I was 40 years old that I was able to really buckle down and begin to learn the language. Don't tell me you can't teach an old dog new tricks! I am now able to sign many worship songs and can communicate with the deaf on a very elementary level. The timing had to be right for my plan of action to make my dream a reality. I dreamed, planned, started the journey, and paused the journey but eventually reached some success many years later—when the time was right. Now, I have set myself a schedule to learn a little bit more every week!

The Prize: WHAT WILL YOU DO WHEN YOU GET THERE?

he wonderful thing about goals is hopefully . . . someday, you will reach them. You can earn your degree(s), write your book, travel the world, learn a second language (even at 40!), or do whatever is in your heart to accomplish. When you have crossed the long-awaited finish line, *don't forget to celebrate!* It is a very important step in the process. I once heard a lady in a conference say that she told her three children, "If you graduate high school without being involved in sex, drugs, or alcohol, I will give you the college of your choice, the car of my choice, and a wedding to remember." All three met their goals and celebrated by attending, and graduating from, the college of their choice while driving a great car—paid for! Now, they all are married and have the pictures to remember their own wedding. That's what I call a celebration on multiple levels!

Celebrations, in and of themselves, are very needed but should not preclude the need to press on even further, to gain and do more. In other words, party and celebrate but set another goal. Keep striving. Keep achieving. Always keep progressing. Don't rest on your past laurels. What God did in a revival a few years ago or even in services last Sunday might have been great, but keep pressing and expecting more. Permanent rest is only granted when you enter the place of permanent rest—Heaven!

Don't mistake your accomplishments as being the end of your journey. You are not finished; you've only just begun!

Footnote:

"Beautiful feet, beautiful feet, tried and true-tiful feet, do
you have beautiful feet?"

4

Footings

MY ISSUE: *MOLDED LIKE CLAY AND BUILT WITH FAITH*

Randy and I, along with our beautiful family, live in the wonderful state of Georgia. Even though neither one of us are natives of Georgia, we have always felt at home here. As with every place, there are certain things I love and others which are not so becoming. For instance, I love the weather in the fall and spring, but the summer humidity is dreadful. I love the mild winters but do not enjoy the endless cold rain. Something everyone is supposed to like is the famous Georgia red clay . . . but not me. It's very hard to dig when the ground is dry, and the beautiful red stain it leaves on your clothes is something pure bleach can't even begin to touch. Maybe if you had the time and were willing to take the risk, hydrochloric acid when applied with a small brush would remove part of the blemish, but who has the time for that? Surely not me (unless, of course, it was on a nice dress or a pair of Prada's).

Another quality of the Georgia red clay is that it sticks to everything it touches. If you walk around in the wet mud, you will quickly be wearing five-pound, red clay shoes on each foot. Walk in bare feet and your toes and toenails will be stained the color of the clay. It may look interesting in the beginning, but getting red clay stains off your feet or shoes is nearly impossible. Take my word on it!

For as much as this renowned natural resource can ruin your clothes, Georgia red clay is a wonderful surface for structural foundations. Now I'm not claiming to be Bob the Builder, but living through a few building projects can teach you quite a bit if you are willing to learn. Whenever a builder begins a structure he must first clear the land and dig the "footings" for the foundation. These are very important as they will determine just how much the entire foundation can hold. In nearly every place, most contractors will use concrete and steel due to the load placed upon the footings. (See, I told you I watched!) But here, they use Georgia red clay. It is as hard as most rocks and usually requires heavy equipment to move or bust. The strong clay produces strong footings and foundations, even without tons of fill dirt for surface preparation.

Made From Clay

Isn't it amazing how God can use something I, personally, really do not care for (like Georgia red dirt) and compare me to it? Well, He didn't particularly use the term "red clay," but the Bible says I am like clay in the Potter's hand.

"Yet, O Lord, you are our Father. We are the clay, you

are the potter; we are all the work of your hand."

ISAIAH 64:8 (NIV)

I am daily being molded and formed by the Master Potter. I figure if God can make something so beneficial out of Georgia red clay, then there is still hope for me!

It's amazing to understand the various properties and grades of clay with which potters can work. Clay is just a lump of mud and water, until someone starts working with it. There are impurities which must first be removed. Then, the clay is dug, washed, mashed, and watered. It requires much preparation before it can even be placed on the potter's wheel. When it is ready for use, the potter decides whether he will shape it by using a wheel or only his bare hands. The process is timely and requires much attention to detail. When the mold is complete to the potter's specifications, it is then put into the fire. The temperature will differ depending on the determined use of the object. If it is undercooked or overcooked, the vessel may not be suitable for its intended purpose.

When I look at myself, I have a lot of the qualities of clay. I, too, am just mud and water until the Master Potter begins His work on me. The impurities in my life must be taken out; and I, too, must go through a purging process which includes being dug, washed, mashed, watered, and finally prepared. None of this is easy; and in some cases, some of the old stuff requires power equipment to be removed! Sometimes, the foundation is dug deeper because the structure must be prepared to withstand more stress. Only the Master really knows what He is making of me. He knows whether to use the potter's wheel or just His hands. He knows just the right time to put me in the fire and the correct temperature I will be able to withstand in order to make of me what He intends. Job 33:6 says it this way:

> *"Behold, I belong to God like you; I too have been*
> *formed out of the clay."*

According to Jeremiah 18:6, God is the Potter who is molding me into His image. He has a right over me, which belongs to no one else, to use me for whatever He desires. Some days, it might be for something honorable; another day, for something common. I may be elevated one day and cleaning toilets the next. The key to being used by the Potter is to be flexible, moldable, and easily shapeable. Whatever is placed in my jar—the gifts deemed good for me—will depend on the anointing of the Holy Spirit and my receptive heart.

Everyone begins the same way, but how we are formed into His image lies in the hands of the Potter.

> *". . . does not the potter have a right over the clay, to*
> *make from the same lump one vessel for honorable use*
> *and another for common use?"*

ROMANS 9:21

How many times have you heard a piece of clay scream at the potter, "I don't want to be an outside pot! I want to be a dinner plate!" Never! But yet, as Christians, we always want to tell God what we think is best for us. We aren't pliable in His hands. Instead, we tell Him how we should be made and what to do with us when He is finished. As we mature, we have a better understanding of what Isaiah 64:8 says:

> *". . . all of us are the work of Your hand."*

Digging it Out

*B*eing in the ministry, there are times we all get tired of doing what we are doing. We feel like we have given until there is nothing left to give, and our strength is totally zapped. Everyone wants a little piece of our time and our lives. Being pulled from every direction drains our spiritual energy and elevates our frustration level to where our response to people is not particularly Christ-like. During these times, it is especially important that we guard the Spirit of God in our lives and continue to fill it with His presence.

· ·

As Christians, we always want to tell God what we think is best for us. We aren't pliable in His hands.

· ·

One of the most difficult challenges as the wife of a minister is having people think you know everything about everything. Wow, don't I wish that was the truth! In reality, we are all creatures made by God and have a commitment to follow the course He has ordained for each of us. Too often, we forget that in order to follow the plan, there are certain things we must do. It is so dangerous to think just because you are "in the ministry" means you have "arrived" at a spiritual place and can stop growing. Nothing can be further from

. . . .

It is so dangerous to think just because you are "in the ministry" means you have "arrived" at a spiritual place and can stop growing.

. . . .

the truth. A ministry position, which is helping people to have a better relationship with God, was never intended to be substituted as your personal, daily relationship with Jesus. Your relationship with Jesus should inspire others to want more of Him. Before you were in the ministry, you were first and foremost a daughter of God. Learning to be a daughter and to better know your Father will transform you into a better woman, wife, mother, and leader.

Take a look in the spiritual mirror of your life. What are you reflecting? What do you see? Are you willing for others to see the same reflection? Or, is it something that brings you shame? Is your spiritual life growing or stagnant? Trust me, at some point in time, we have all substituted the work of the ministry for our personal walk with God. Some catch it, repent, and fall in love with Jesus all over again, not just the ministry. Sadly, others do not realize their deception until they are either spiritually desolate or living a life of sin. No matter what your life is reflecting at this moment, always keep these desires in front of you concerning your personal relationship with God.

Stay Hungry . . . For the Right Things

One of my favorite scriptures in the Bible is Matthew 5:6 (NIV):

> *"Blessed are those who hunger and thirst for righteousness, for they will be filled."*

Having a hunger after God is different than hungering after physical things. I once knew a lady who had a serious hunger problem—not for food, but for STUFF! Anytime I would see her, the first words out of her mouth were, "Girl, let me tell you what I just got me!" Nothing could ever satisfy her. No matter how much stuff she accumulated, she always wanted more and needed more. She would buy a new dress, wear it once, then say it just didn't fit correctly; thus, opening the door for yet another new dress. I watched her buy all of the latest exercise equipment only to give it away two months later. Her life contained a deep vacuum because she was hungering after stuff that could never satisfy. She had made a commitment to Christ, but never gave any priority to developing her relationship with Him. Filling her life with STUFF only made her hungrier and eventually, emptier. These things she craved were not sinful; they just never could satisfy her. In her pursuit of satisfaction and fulfillment, she missed the one thing—the only thing—which could fill her need: a relationship with Jesus Christ, not a mere acquaintance. The lust of her flesh resulted in a vacuum in her spirit. The Bible teaches exactly what we should be hungry and searching after:

> *"So I say, live by the Spirit, and you will not gratify the desires of the sinful nature. For the sinful nature desires*

what is contrary to the Spirit, and the Spirit what is contrary to the sinful nature. They are in conflict with each other, so that you do not do what you want."

GALATIANS 5:16-17 (NIV)

"In a well-furnished kitchen there are not only crystal goblets and silver platters, but waste cans and compost buckets—some containers used to serve fine meals, others to take out the garbage. Become the kind of container God can use to present any and every kind of gift to his guests for their blessing. Run away from infantile indulgence. Run after mature righteousness— faith, love, peace—joining those who are in honest and serious prayer before God."

2 TIMOTHY 2:20-22 (MSG)

Have you ever been really, physically hungry, but for all the wrong things? You know, the times where it seems no matter how much you eat, you still crave more? During those times, if you love salty foods, all the sunflower seeds in the world couldn't curb your appetite. For the person with a sweet tooth, Ding Dongs® would chase Twinkies®, which would chase cup cakes, which would chase fruit pies—and it's never enough. You crave that with which you fill your life.

A few years ago, I felt impressed of the Holy Spirit to go on a chocolate fast during the season of Lent. I had never before acknowledged or celebrated Lent, except for this particular year. I knew my love for chocolate but never really the extent of my endearment. During the first few days of this journey, I found myself thinking about chocolate, dreaming about chocolate, smelling non-existent chocolate, being offered chocolate everywhere we went, and even found myself with chocolate candy in my hand without realizing what I was doing. Chocolate had become a very important part of my life and now it was gone for 40 days. Lord, help me! Easter could not come soon enough! I knew once it had passed, I could indulge into my chocolate craze again. As the days went by, I discovered how chocolate was losing its hold on my life. It was amazing to see how I had lost my cravings. Easter passed, and I no longer felt my day was incomplete without some kind of chocolate. That bondage had been broken in me. Today, I still enjoy a good chocolate dessert; but sometimes, I will choose cherry pie over chocolate pie. This also taught me how to be very selective about the types of chocolate I enjoy!

The responsibility to develop your hunger for God, for His presence and His holiness, is yours and yours alone.

Before my fast, I was craving the very thing with which was filling my life. Spiritual hunger is much the same way. When you are in the presence of God, you begin to desire more and more of God. With spiritual hunger, the more you commune with Jesus, the more you want. You cannot be satisfied with the mundane. The realization comes alive that there must be more than what you have, and you begin to search and develop your hunger for more of God.

The responsibility to develop your hunger for God, for His presence and His holiness, is yours and yours alone. It cannot be done for you. If God seems far away, guess who moved? Not God! The Bible says that when you draw close to Him, He will draw close to you (see James 4:8). In your quest for more of Him, let these few things help your appetite to grow.

1. **Search for God with your whole desire.** Nothing should come before God and your relationship with Him—not even the ministry! Ten times in Psalms, David conveys his desire to know God and to worship Him with his whole heart, his entire being. A couple of my favorites are:

    ". . . And besides You, I desire nothing on earth."

    PSALM 73:25B (NASB)

    ". . . my soul thirsts for You, my flesh yearns for You . . ."

    PSALM 63:1

2. **Be diligent and consistent.** When you are diligent in your search for God, you will not only search but also find that His Word is real in your life. Applying His Word allows you to become more consistent in your walk with Him. Diligence brings devotion to the things of God, and devotion brings the ability to persevere in the toughest of circumstances.

"All Judah rejoiced about the oath because they had sworn it wholeheartedly. They sought God eagerly, and he was found by them. So the LORD gave them rest on every side."

2 Chronicles 15:15 (NIV)

Hebrews 11:6 says that God rewards those who diligently seek Him. His desire is to have people who are whole-hearted, not half-hearted. When you are whole-hearted and diligent, He provides rest and reward. I don't know about you, but I can always use a little more rest and a bit more reward.

3. **Spend time at the table eating the Bread of Life.** In other words, take time for your devotions and your personal Bible study. Dig into the Word of God to find more about Him. Learn about His love for you and His plans for your life. Remember, it cannot happen *through* you until it has happened *to* you. It is not necessary to have a great revelation. Learn to know Him first. As you spend time with God eating His spiritual food, revelations will come, and you will have more to pour out of your life into the lives of others.

Begin to Bear Fruit

W hen you learn to abide in Christ and fill your hunger with more and more of Jesus, it is inevitable you will begin to bear fruit. This will be real fruit, not things which resemble fruit but

· ·

Remember, it cannot happen through you until it has happened to you.

· ·

have no substance or longevity. The problem with fruit is that it sometimes has pits. No one likes to eat pits because they are usually very bitter. And sometimes, they show up when you least expect them.

A few years ago, we moved into a new house that needed some landscaping. In the fall of that year, I decided a few ornamental trees would be just perfect in our front yard. So, I went tree shopping and purchased a couple of red maple trees and a weeping cherry tree. Randy and I planted those beautiful trees in the ground and were very anxious to see a lovely spring bloom. Sure enough, spring came and all of our new trees were loaded with blossoms. Spring turned into summer and the blooms fell off and leaves sprouted. Everything was going according as planned. However, within a short time, something went wrong with my weeping cherry tree. The limbs began to wilt and hang toward the ground as if it was diseased. I was greatly troubled about this unexpected turn of events and decided to investigate it more closely. Imagine my surprise when I approached my ornamental cherry tree and found it covered in peaches! "How in the world did this thing get peaches?" I asked myself. "It's supposed to be a cherry tree!" Then it dawned on me. It had been mislabeled when it was dormant and transplanted to our yard.

Now, I have nothing against peach trees. After all, I live in

Georgia, the peach capital of the world! I just didn't want a peach tree in my front yard, mainly because of the pits they produce. They are huge, unsightly, and hurt when you step on them with bare feet. But like it or not, I had bought, planted, and now had a peach tree. I could have stood over that tree all summer and said, "Listen here, tree, you are a cherry tree!" and it would not have changed its God-given character.

During the first summer of growth, I had to place a lot of time into the care of my new, little peach tree to make sure the pests didn't destroyed it. It took a lot of work to see that my new tree had a good root system and was properly grounded. As it grew and matured, I had to battle different things than I did the first year, but it was all part of the process.

Now, several years later, I like my peach tree! You see, it bears fruit. An ornamental cherry tree is just that—ornamental. It does not bear real or even pretend fruit. Each year, we enjoy the succulent peaches which would not have grown if we had not planted that peach tree. It still requires pruning, watering, fertilizer to ensure its growth, and protection from pests, not to mention having to mess with all the pits on the ground. But, a sweet and juicy, fresh-picked peach on a summer's night makes it all worth while!

Your spiritual life is much the same way. Little pests can destroy your spiritual growth if your root system is not grounded in the Word of God. The battles you faced as a young believer are different than those you encounter as you mature in God. Things which, at one time brought you to the point of failure, will no longer be able to do as you grow past that point of difficulty. You just fight a different pest.

Bearing good fruit is one of the most fulfilling parts of the Christian life. The problem is, sometimes we all have to deal with the pits and the pain which bearing fruit can bring. Who likes to be pruned? Watered? Fertilized? Actually, no one that I know. But, it is all part of the process to ensure more fruit and longevity. No one knows the entire harvest that will come into their lives, or how many trees will take root from the seeds they have planted. However, these things are for certain: you have been called, you have been planted, you are a fruit-bearing tree by nature, and you are designed to bring forth much fruit!

Guard What You Put Into Your Soul

The things which fill your life will be the things you think about most often. Your abiding time becomes your bearing time. If you are constantly watching soap operas and reading romance novels, guess what? You will be thinking about unhealthy relationships and be swept away by fantasies. Are you bearing the goodness of Jesus? Or, are you reaping a different kind of harvest? To know God and His characteristics only comes from intimate times with the Father.

I can tell you a few things about Elvis: where he was born, lived, and died. I can sing you some of his music and tell you a few of his movies. There's probably enough information I've collected

Your abiding time becomes your bearing time.

SECTION II: *Family Issues*

Footnote:

"How lovely on the mountains are the feet of them that bring good news."

Isaiah 52:7

5

Mismates

My Issue: Marital Relationships

Walk into some shoe stores, and immediately you feel as though they have gone out of their way to make it difficult for a woman to try on shoes. First of all, they strap shoes together with a cableties making it possible to try on only one shoe at a time. It looks ridiculous to walk across the store while dragging one shoe behind you. And of course, the shoe you are trying on usually will have a different heel height than the shoe you wore into the store, which makes you walk with a pronounced limp across the floor, with one leg three inches shorter than the other. Walking with a limp and a drag does have a tendency to make people stop and stare.

Another method is using the old security tag. I'm not talking about the little metal plate which sets off the alarms when you walk out the door. No, it's the big, ugly tag used to bolt the two shoes together. To remove this tag, you must first find a clerk who is willing to find the tool necessary to remove the tag, allowing you to slip your little foot into the second shoe. This is usually accompanied by the clerk's obvious irritation, as they observe your every move while huffing and puffing, making sure you do not walk out of the store with their precious shoes. But you cannot fully concentrate on important issues like getting a proper view of the way the shoe looks from various angles or the way it feels as you walk; because as soon as you take your foot out of the shoe, the tag is quickly re-inserted into the sides of the shoe. All this to discourage you from even asking for a second try, if indeed those were the pair you liked the best. Oh, and don't forget the little holes from the security tag which are now embedded in your new pair of shoes. And if you ask about them, the patented answer is something like, "The tags are a necessary part of our security procedure. Don't worry though, those little holes will go away after you wear the shoes a few times." Yeah, right. Spontaneous shoe healing!

After you have finally endured the process of making your decision on the right pair of shoes, now it's time to pay. That's easy, right? Wrong! First, you are asked if you would like to "automatically save an additional 10%" by signing up for the in-store credit card (which charges you 25% interest. Hmm . . . Where's the "good deal" there?) Then, you find out they only accept debit or credit cards—no checks, unless you are willing to offer your first-born as collateral.

Once you give the sweet clerk a charge card, they begin to inspect your purchase. Most of the time, they are checking the box for MISMATES! They must be in the proper box with identical stock numbers on the sole. Both shoes must be the same length, color, and size. Heavens, it is a pair of shoes, not a key into the Pentagon!

All of this drama is a little overdone because to buy a pair of shoes deliberately mismated is ludicrous. Have you ever tried to wear two different sizes of shoes at the same time . . . on purpose? I'm sure many of us have tried on different shoes while making a decision as to which ones looks better with a particular outfit but, hopefully, not in public. My feet, just like my legs, are on the same body and have received the messages to grow at the same rate, resulting in them being the same size. Some may argue that their genetics and DNA have produced two different sized feet—for which I have sympathy. But for me, I want two shoes, the same size, for my same-sized feet!

Resist the Urge!

I, like many other women looking for the "deal of the century," have gone into some stores selling mismatched shoes. Even though the savings are great (for obvious reasons!), I just can't bring myself to buying one of those discounted pair. If my feet are slightly different, they are definitely not enough to merit two completely different sizes of shoes. Hopefully, no woman reading this would have the nerve to try to slip out of a store with two different-sized shoes. Women of the same-sized feet, let's band together! Think about the shopper behind you who just might be needing the size eight, left shoe that you walked out of the store with (along with the seven and a half right shoe!). Pray, "Lord, lead us not into temptation to purchase two different-sized shoes." Resist the urge—stay the course!

Soul Mates, Not Mismates

Even though the whole issue of mismates, as it relates to shoes, can be one which produces much frustration, it pales in comparison to real life mismates. Thus, my issue for this chapter: marital relationships. Now, I'm not saying I'm Dr. Gary Smalley or Dr. Phil, but I am deeply concerned with the havoc the devil is playing—now more than ever—on ministry marriages. As I said before, perception is not reality. Quite often, minister's wives live a public "perfect" marriage; while behind closed doors, they are in a very dysfunctional relationship, striving daily just to survive. Whether this describes your marriage or if you live in "heaven-on-earth," I believe these next few pages will be an encouragement for you and for your mate.

The man to whom I am married, Randy Valimont, is my sole mate and soul mate—not my mismate mate. Some people try on husbands much like they try on shoes. Not me. After much prayer and contemplation, Randy is the one I chose, and he chose me. He's not perfect, but neither am I. He may not seem like a perfect fit at times, but he is truly the correct mate for me and all of my mismatched issues.Ou r feet continue to travel the same paths together even though, at times, it feels as though we are only held together by a cable or security tag! Then, there are those moments when one of us is dragging the other behind, or it feels like one of our heels is higher than the other. But no matter what the issue or circumstance, no amount of difficulty in life would be worth leaving him to try on another. I've just about got him broken in and to find another perfect fit would be way too much work!

Ground Zero: The Call

*I*f you are reading this book, you are probably already involved in some area of ministry either as a minister in your own right, the spouse of a minister, or you're considering marrying someone who feels the call of God into the ministry. If you are married, you have dual commitments—one to your marriage, the other to the ministry. If you are not married, you may be only committed to ministry. In either case, there must be a fear and reverence for the call of God on your life and that of your spouse. It will be imperative for you to understand this call and its eternal significance.

The call of God will bring every imaginable hurt and conceivable victory. Through the years, I have asked various ministers and their wives to describe in simple words what the ministry has been like for them. Their responses have been as varied as the ministers themselves. I have heard descriptions like: "lonely," "overwhelming," "guarded," "painful," "tiring," and "two steps from hell." But I've also had some describe the ministry as "being loved and protected," "encouraging;" and "just like heaven." Some struggle looking for the magic formula with all the right answers while facing unrealistic expectations. Others seem to never miss a beat and have a great church, effective ministry, and a strong marriage. The truth is, all of these responses are a mirror of life itself.

Face it. We all go through the same things at different times. What sets us apart is that we have been marked by the call of God and set apart for "such a time as this" (see Esther 4:13-15).

We know we are doing the very thing God has placed in our hearts and can do nothing else. To understand the "the call of God" and its importance is imperative for a minister and his family. Sometimes, just knowing you are doing exactly what God has called you to do can be your only saving grace. But, you are not alone. There have been many before you whom God called; and at times, that calling was their only hope. Take a look at a few examples.

MOSES

Here was a prince among the Egyptians who, for some reason, God set apart for a special time. Pharaoh's daughter found Moses floating in a basket but gave him back to his biological mother to nurse him until he was older. During this time, she had the opportunity to instill the fear and reverence of Almighty God into him, teach him the ways of his people, and tell Moses many times how God spared his life. This undoubtedly gave him hope for what God had planned for his future.

Do you remember how God called Moses? Through a burning bush. I can imagine Moses looking back on this divine experience many times to keep himself anchored in God's divine work. In the same way, when times get tough, we need to remember an epiphany in our lives—our own "burning bush" experience—removing all doubt that we are doing the very thing God has called us to do.

SAMUEL

Samuel was the first-born child of a woman who was supposed to be barren. God heard her many prayers and blessed her with a child of promise. At the proper age, Samuel was given to the priests to serve in the house of the Lord.

JEREMIAH

Jeremiah was called "the weeping prophet." He was ordained to call God's people back into a right relationship with Him. God knew Jeremiah before he was ever born, and He had set him apart for a specific work. In Jeremiah 1:4-8, God spoke directly to Jeremiah and placed a definitive call upon his life:

> " . . . *The word of the Lord came to me saying,*
> *'Before I formed you in the womb I knew you, and*
> *before you were born I consecrated you; I appointed*
> *you a prophet to the nations.'"*

JEREMIAH 1:4-5

But Jeremiah, just like Moses and many others God has called, had his list of why he thought he could not measure up to such a high calling:

> *"'Ah, Sovereign Lord,' I said, 'I do not know*
> *how to speak; I am only a child.' But the Lord*
> *said to me, 'Do not say, "I am only a child." You*
> *must go to everyone I send you to and say whatever*
> *I command you. Do not be afraid of them, for*
> *I am with you and will rescue you,' declares the*
> *Lord."*

JEREMIAH 1: 6-8 (NIV)

God explained to Jeremiah that He would be with him, regardless of his circumstances or self-imposed limitations. Jeremiah did not understand how or when God would fulfill the covenant He had made with Abraham, but he had to learn to trust that God would fulfill His word.

JESUS' DISCIPLES

In the New Testament, Jesus called His 12 disciples by using two words: "Follow me."[1] Upon hearing these two simple words, they immediately left their families, professions, and businesses and began to follow Jesus. The most intriguing thing is Jesus never told them where they were going! They had no idea their journey would not only be three years of discipleship training, but a lifetime of following Jesus—even unto their death.

How many times over those three years did they say, "What have we done? What have we gotten ourselves into?" I'm sure plenty of times. But the call from the Master overrode all fear, doubt, and discouragement.

SAUL OF TARSUS

In Acts chapter nine, there was a man whose government job was to oversee the persecutions and ultimate death of Christians. His name was Saul. Saul was on his mission, but God had other plans. While traveling on a road to the city of Damascus, God finally got Saul's attention by knocking him off his horse, blinding his eyes, and speaking directly from heaven to him. From that day forward, we have no record of Saul, who became Paul, ever turning his back from following God. In fact, he wrote two-thirds of the New Testament and became the greatest apostle to ever live.

So, why all of the drama and theatrics? It's simple. God knew Paul would face much discouragement and would need a strong reference point of how God supernaturally placed His call on his life. And, it worked because even through horrific persecution, Paul never walked away from his ministry.

---

1 See John 1:43

As a minister of the Gospel, you are called of God: set apart, with a special anointing, to do a special task. Maybe you are like Paul and can pinpoint a certain time or miraculous event when you knew God called you into the ministry. On the other hand, you may be like Samuel and might not recall a certain time or place, but you know God has placed a special anointing on your life. You may not even know exactly what that call may be. Here is something to always remember: God is sovereign, and He can choose anyone at anytime, in anyway to do a special work. This doesn't mean it makes you "special." It simply means that God can use a donkey to speak if He chooses.[2]

God is sovereign, and He can choose anyone at anytime, in anyway to do a special work.

Even though every Christian has a divine purpose in God, not everyone is destined to full-time ministry. Some are called to work part-time while others are called to volunteer or to be available to use their gifts for special projects. The Bible says, *"For many are called, but few are chosen"* (Matthew 22:14). God has not placed His call on your life due to your merit; it is because of your lack of worth. He anoints and chooses the least likely, so they will have no right to claim any accolades belonging to God.

---

2 See Numbers 22:21-34

We do have to guard against letting someone other than God call us into full-time ministry. There are so many well-meaning saints who think they know God's plan for you and everyone else. Some of them are so determined for you to fulfill their—not God's—plan, they may try to equip you financially, or academically to follow the road into ministry. Usually, when all else fails, they revert to their ace-in-the-hole: the prophetic word! For surely, if anyone starts a sentence by saying, "Thus saith the Lord . . . ," then it MUST be straight from God, right? Not so fast! A word of knowledge concerning God's will for your life will always bear witness and confirm what God has already told you. When God places a ministry call on your life, you will know it. If you are in the ministry just because Sister So-and-So told you it was what you were supposed to do, it may be time to re-evaluate! Ask yourself the question, "Can I truly be happy doing something else?" If your answer is, "Yes!" then go do it. The return of our Lord is upon us, and this is the time when ministers cannot be divided in their loyalties.

It breaks my heart whenever I see so many people leaving their place of ministry for so many different reasons. Some have been overwhelmed with discouragement, even to the point of divorce and suicide. Still, others have not experienced the success some others have (Never compare yourself with someone else—YOU WILL

This life of ministry can be lived with joy and peace.

ALWAYS LOSE!) Then, there have been those who have allowed sin to invade their lives. The list goes on and on. Many of the people I have spoken with told me that if they could do it all again, they would follow God and yield to His call on their lives, regardless of what they thought it might cost them. Now, they have the sadness of leaving their calling, and they live with regrets . . . daily.

Let me ask you a couple of questions. When your life is finished, will you look back through the years and change nothing? Knowing what you know now, would you wish you had done something else beside ministry? I want to encourage you that this life of ministry can be lived with joy and peace. Sure, you will walk hand-in-hand with suffering and sorrow, but it is through these times, you learn what it truly means to commit all your ways to Him (Psalm 37:4-6).

"You Can Back Out Now!"

*R*andy and I were both attending Southeastern College in Lakeland, Florida when we became engaged. Many of our peers were getting married, and it seemed to be the logical conclusion to our time in school. I figured I was getting the best of both worlds: coming out of college with both my B.A. and "Mrs." degrees! As we planned the wedding, we decided to put a unique twist on our wedding invitations. Because we were entering into ministry, we invited our loved ones to come and witness the "joining of two hearts in marriage and ministry." Although we both felt a strong call into ministry, until that time, I had never really thought about the idea of joining our ministries together.

Our wedding day approached with all of the excitement, fun,

and inevitable difficulties of any wedding couple. I will never forget standing in the foyer, waiting with my father to walk me down the aisle and join my new husband. I was a nervous wreck! The organist was playing the wedding march, the doors were closed, my mother was seated; the entire wedding party was in place. All we were missing was for the bride to walk down the aisle. My dad looked at me with tears in his eyes and said, "You know, honey, you can back out now if you want to . . ." Seeing I was the first in my immediate family to marry, I thought Daddy was just having a hard time letting go . . . until he spoke his next words: "You need to understand that you can back out now; but once you walk down the aisle and join Randy in marriage, there is no turning back. Right now, you would just be walking away from a man; but if you change your mind later, you will be walking away from a ministry, and you will answer to God." My lightning-fast mind spun a quick calculation. I knew the love Randy and I had for one another and for God would be enough to withstand the trials of our ministry, and we would grow together. Then and there, I settled the age-old question of commitment. The doors opened, the crowd stood, the cameras flashed, and my dad proudly walked me down the aisle to join my new husband.

Before we were married, there was never a question of what we would do if this "ministry thing" didn't work out. There was not a plan "b." We took the vow of not parting each other OR the ministry except through death, and we knew the seriousness of our vows.

Getting to Know You

Our wedding was glorious, and everyone was so happy, including Randy and me. We KNEW we had made the absolute right decision for us and our future. We enjoyed our honeymoon like all other newlyweds. (And yes, even ministers can have great sex!) Soon, our life was off and running. I was singing, "Nothing but blue skies from now on!"

It didn't take very long until Randy and I realized we didn't have as much in common as we had originally thought. I was raised in a family of all girls; Randy was raised with all boys. He knew nothing about estrogen, and I knew nothing about testosterone—which was unfortunate because I had a lot of estrogen, and he had a lot of testosterone! That combination did make for some good fireworks! He yelled, and I pouted. He wanted to save every dime we had while I wanted to spend a little on extravagances. There were times I wanted to walk away; and I'm sure on many occasions, Randy was ready to run away. However, we realized early in our marriage our commitment to each other was for life. Quitting was never—and has never been—an option.

· ·

Marriage is a lifetime journey.

· ·

Our marriage has neither been a continuous honeymoon nor a non-stop battle. Marriage is a lifetime journey. No one just wakes up one day and figures, "Hey I know how to be married for life" and all of a sudden everything just falls into place. There are no quick fixes to the issues of life as they pertain to marriage. Walking away is not the answer. Getting tough is.

Marriage and Ministry

*R*andy and I went into our marriage knowing the call of God on our lives was forever. Just as marriage is a lifetime journey, so is the ministry. You don't magically wake up one day and all of a sudden have all the answers. Just when you think you have it figured out, something comes along out of nowhere, or someone says something devastating to your spirit that you never saw coming. (In the South we call this getting "sucker punched.") Once again, you have no answers. About the time you start teaching on finances, the bottom drops out of your own. When "Living by Faith" is the title for your next series of messages, someone will be diagnosed with an incurable disease or a barren woman calls needing encouragement because she's still not pregnant this month. Ministry is a lifetime of learning, growing, and changing your ideas to help meet the needs of God's people for a particular time.

Like it or not, when you are in ministry, you are a leader! People look to their pastors and ministers to lead them into the deeper truths of a relationship with God. As leaders, we all must answer to a higher call, a greater sacrifice. We cannot allow ourselves the "luxury" of walking away when walking forward seems too difficult. God requires a higher level of accountability for those called into leadership. Luke 12:48 says that anyone who has been given much, much will be required. One of the basic requirements Paul writes to Timothy, a young pastor overseeing a very large church, is he must have his relationships and family life in order. Paul writes it this way:

"One who rules his own house well, having his children in submission with all reverence (for if a man does not

*know how to rule his own house, how will he take care
of the church of God?)"*

1 TIMOTHY 3:4-5 (NKJV)

Marriage within itself is difficult. Ministry is difficult. When you add marriage and ministry, you have a great opportunity for amazing success or debilitating failure. Only you can decide what it will be. As for me, I have chosen to walk the difficult road and become significant in God's call for my life.

Dealing with Conflict

So, now you're married. And let me guess, no one ever told you married life could be so wonderful and so difficult at the same time, right? You have left the home of your parents, hopefully, and set up your own household. Life is just as you always thought it would be until that first little irritation comes along or maybe the first really big argument. Conflict is inevitable. Remember, you didn't marry someone who was just like you. What would be the point? But when two people from two diverse backgrounds come together in martial bliss, there will be disagreements, even the dreaded "argument" on occasion. "You mean ministers argue with their spouses?" I said we were "called," not "angelic beings!"

Your immediate response to conflict will vary depending on three things:

1. **How have you handled past arguments?** Have you drawn clear lines of communication and learned how to

settle conflicts within Godly parameters? Have you agreed to disagree? Or, have you walked away and called your best friend—or worse, your "prayer partner"? Do you resolve conflict by running home to your parents to complain about this horrible person you are married to?

2. **How did your parents handle conflict?** Did they set healthy guidelines for you? Did you see things you don't want to repeat in your relationship?

3. **How do you want to resolve conflict in your married lives?** Do you always want to have someone else to settle your conflicts? How do you want your children to settle theirs in school, at home, and in their married life?

So many of the things you do during those first months and years of marriage set the tone for your entire future together. When you learn to communicate clearly and settle issues between you and your spouse, you are on the road to a healthy relationship.

Sometimes, conflicts are of such great proportion they do need intervention. If this occurs, don't let the false pride of having the "perfect ministry marriage" keep you from finding help. Of course, it doesn't have to be broadcast throughout the church that, "Pastor and his wife are fighting so much that they are going to counseling!" Keep it private between you and your spouse. Find a Godly, Christ-centered person or counseling service which can help you according to the standards in the Word of God. Be careful, though, that you are not just looking for someone else to settle your conflicts for you. Not only is this unhealthy, but it is also a sign of an immature person and an immature relationship.

Always Keep Building and Re-Building

*W*hen you and your husband began dating or courting, there were things you did to build your relationship to the point where you thought you would be compatible for marriage. Regardless of how long you have been married, sometimes we need to go back and examine those beginnings. Remembering and reflecting is not a bad thing as long as we do not live in the past. You can never go back to those days, but you can revisit them occasionally and do some of those things which made you fall in love in the first place. You can also keep your relationship fresh by doing some new things that will help you and your spouse fall more in love with one another.

1. **Make the most of whatever drew you together in the first place.** Whether it was studying, talking, playing, watching movies, picnics, eating out occasionally, or just looking into one another's eyes. Find the time to do it again. If you cannot find the time, then make the time for it.

2. **Set a specific time for reflection.** Do you have a conference, convention, or meeting you attend every year? If so, start to make it more than just another ministry event. Take some time together (preferably without kids!) and talk about your year together—WITH NO MINISTRY INCLUDED! In other words, this is not the time to discuss church budgets or who left the church over the past year. Those things will come and go. Take time to revisit your year together. What were the highlights, the low points, and the surprising, funny, or disappointing things that happened? Don't forget to include your sex life in this conversation!

3. **Be spontaneous and innovative.** Everything you do does not have to cost money. A candlelight dinner may not appeal to your husband, but if you are dressed in a negligee, dinner by candlelight could be the best idea you ever had!

Here is a great thought concerning ministry and marriage. Keep it before you constantly and watch God work His will in your life! To be a partner in ministry is to say, "I am called by God. I am not perfect, but I am trying to be like Christ. I may have issues, but I will not walk away from my marriage or my ministry. Even though I may struggle, I will work, and I will succeed."

> *"It is my family God has chosen! Yes, he has made an everlasting covenant with me. His agreement is eternal, final, sealed. He will constantly look after my safety and success."*

> 2 SAMUEL 23:5 (NLT)

Remarriage and Ministry

As you have probably surmised by now, I am in my first—and with God's help—my only marriage. Like I said before, I am of the opinion that it takes entirely too long to break in a pair of new shoes, and entirely too long to train a new husband! "Breaking in" or "training" is not my specialty, but I do know both are painful and take a huge commitment, regardless of the circumstances.

Marriages end for many reasons: the death of a spouse, problems with money, children, infidelity; physical, emotional, or spiritual abuse; drug use, the death of a child, in-law problems, lack of commitment . . . and the list can go on and on. Many of you reading this book will be in a second or maybe even a third marriage. No matter how you slice it, something dies in each party when a marriage is ended, for whatever the reason. One common area for ministers and their spouses to deal with is God's divine plan and call for their lives. They really feel as though they have messed it all up; and now God cannot use them because of their marital failures.

* *

God can use anyone at any time with any issues.

* *

Allow me to reassure you: God can use anyone at any time with any issues. Divorce is not the unforgivable sin. In the past, Christian ministries have made divorcees feel like their chance for ministry has passed them by. On the other hand, many today have sugar-coated failures in marriage as being a product of society. Ministers in this day and age change spouses as much as some do shirts, and keep right on moving, never considering the consequences of their own spiritual well-being and emotional stability. Neither of these scenarios are correct.

I believe there must be a balance. As ministers of the Gospel of Jesus Christ, we cannot dismiss the gifts and the call of a person just because he or she may have been married and remarried. If God has called a person, who are we to say that he or she is not worthy of the call? On the other hand, we cannot allow people to throw away their marriages just as they would throw away an old pair of shoes. If a person repeatedly walks away from marriage and its commitments, there obviously is a much deeper problem.

God is a God of creation and re-creation. If God can create love, He can re-create love in a broken relationship. Allow me to give you an example. Many years ago, a pastor left his wife and family for another woman. He married the other woman and went into another pastoral position in another state. His first wife stayed single for more than 30 years, believing God for the restoration of her marriage and for her family. During her years alone, she taught a Sunday School class, raised her children to love and follow the plan of God, and personally lived a Godly, successful life. As time passed, the pastor's second wife became ill and died. In a supreme act of restoration, God brought the pastor and his first wife back together to live out their twilight years as husband and wife. Was it God's plan for this all to happen? Probably not. Did God use all of the circumstances to bring about His Glory? Yes, yes, and yes!

I am huge believer of restoration, but I also know there are occasions where restoration is not possible. Above all, never give up, never give in, and never stop believing in the plan God has for your life—regardless of the circumstances.

Never stop believing in the plan God has for your life—regardless of the circumstances.

Footnote:

"It is time for us to get in step with Godly reality."

6

Sexy Shoes

*M*y 17 year-old daughter asked, "Mom, do these shoes make my legs look sexy?" while shopping for the perfect pair to match her Easter suit. The green color was perfect, the four-inch spiked heel was attractive, and the toe was pointed enough to kill a cockroach in a tight corner. All around, they did look really good on her; making her legs look longer and her calf muscles more defined. So, the answer to her question was, "Yes, they do make your legs look sexy." But here within lay the problem: 17 year-old girls—especially the one in my house—are not supposed to look "sexy." So, I did not buy the shoes for her. Instead, I bought them for me. They were perfect with my new negligee!

Oh yeah, there is something else besides sexy Easter shoes that I'm pretty possessive about: *my husband!* And, if you are married to a pastor or minister, you should be as well.

I Have Issues

My Husband, My Life

Even though many people and circumstances would like to tell you differently, your husband is just that—*your husband*. No church function, no meeting, no counseling session, no person—except Jesus Christ—should have priority over you. Over the years, and using a variety of methods, I have had the opportunity to help my husband establish this fact. What helped me the most was teaching a class in our church for young married couples. I studied a wide range of subject matters and found the more knowledgeable I became on the subjects of marriage and fidelity, the better our marriage became. The key for me was not only learning more about the topic of marriage, but then putting forth a conscious effort to have a better marriage. Too many people "know what to do" but fail to put forth any effort whatsoever. Maybe they think their marriage doesn't need any help and fall suspect to the old adage: "If it isn't broke, don't fix it!" Sadly, many marriages—even in ministry homes—are broken and destroyed, without anyone noticing or doing anything about it.

As a minister's wife, not only are you in a marriage, which is a journey in itself, but you are supposed to have an ideal marriage for others to model. To say, "Follow me as I follow Christ," is sometimes very difficult as we have tough times in our own marriages, just like everyone else. But, we also have really good times (at least I pray you do). As I said before, marriage is a mirror of life with its seasons and changes. As much as we—and the people we are in front of every week—want to have sunshine and daisies every day, that world only exists in some fairytale land!

I remember a time when I was very resentful of the church and the ministry. It basically stemmed from my misconception that Randy was more married to the church than he was me. It was a paradoxical situation because I knew we were called, and I could see him flourishing in his ministry to others; but at the same time, I felt deep rejection. Many times I would ask myself, "How can he love them more than me? I thought *I* was supposed to be his first love!" After a long period of self-pity, things finally started to make a turn—*after I began to be a better wife!* It wasn't long until I began to feel as though he was married to me and not to the church. Today, I know beyond any doubt, that I am second in Randy's life, only after his relationship with Jesus Christ. There are many things which follow on his priority list, but I know now where I stand.

Start with the Mirror

Notice, I said these positive changes started to take place in our marriage only *after* I made some significant adjustments and changes. Up until the time I began to look in the mirror, I was placing blame everywhere I could find—on the church, the ministry, Randy, God, Oprah, Dr. Phil, the devil—you name it! But, God got a hold of me, and that's when the tide started to turn.

Here are a few things I began to incorporate in our marriage, which I believe can be of great benefit to you, as well.

1. **Focus on yourself and what you can do to be a better wife.** Find out what you are doing that drives him batty, and change it. Find the things which bring your husband joy and do those more frequently. Develop a style of communication that speaks his language. (Don't expect him to learn yours until you have learned his.) Learn to love unconditionally with a servant attitude. Begin to serve

him and do it well. Ask God to help you become the wife He has called you to be, and the wife your husband needs.

Many years ago, Marabel Morgan wrote a book entitled, *The Total Woman*. This was not one of the books which "completely changed my life," but it did give me some good ideas to think about. One of the things I remember most are the examples she gave of how to be spontaneous and innovative in marriage. At times, being too innovative got her into trouble, but her principles were good. She kept her husband's interest by doing things unexpectedly.

One of the things I read and tried was calling my husband on the phone and talking suggestively to him— when he least expected it. This went great . . . until he realized he had me on speaker phone for everyone else to hear as well! He was a little embarrassed but got over it pretty quickly. (For the sake of my mother, who will probably read this book, I will refrain from any other specific examples.) The principle is: use your God-given creativity and assets to keep your husband interested in you!

2. **Make yourself indispensable to him.** This section could just as easily be called, "Understanding Your Husband's Need for Sex," but again, my mother would pass out! One of the first books I taught in my married couples class was by Dr. Willard F. Harley entitled, *His Needs, Her Needs*. I knew my husband enjoyed sex and seemed to need it, but I never realized it was his *greatest* need until I read this book. Call me ignorant if you want; but the truth is, I just didn't

know. Another thing which was a revelation to me was, in his eyes, affection and sex were synonymous. Now, in my world, those two terms meant two totally different things. As a woman, I had a need for affection, and he had a need for sex. It was amazing to see that once I began to freely meet his sexual needs, he began to understand and meet my need for affection.

When I began to make special time to love and enjoy Randy, he reciprocated it by making extra time for me. A few times in the beginning, I had to remind him, even going so far as writing things down on his calendar. I remember going through his desk and writing random things like, "Bring Jelly a candy bar and a drink," or "Call Jelly today, and tell her how much you love her." My provoking paid off, as now these types of things have become second nature for him, and he remembers all by himself! I still randomly schedule lunches and dinners at unexpected times, in unexpected places. These things do not have to cost a lot of money, but they do require a determination and a desire to do things together. These types of surprises, which are out of your daily routine and grind, can keep you and your spouse connected and bring you back to what brought you to this place in life—your love for one another.

I finally got Randy to realize that he cannot live without me! I am his domestic goddess! When I am gone, he misses me terribly. When he is gone, he cannot wait to return home. He is independently dependent on ME! I give him strokes and build deposits into his emotional and physical bank. He looks to me—not to anyone else—to meet his needs. In fact, if I find out someone is encroaching on my territory of ministry to my husband, they are in serious trouble!

3. **Develop an understanding heart.** If there is one area a minister/husband needs, other than in the sexual arena, it is to have a wife with an understanding heart. There are so many times you will need to not only lift him up in prayer but encourage him verbally, build his spirit, and feed his ego. You will need to listen to his frustrations and his hurts, not demanding more of him than he can give. Regardless how others perceive your husband as "super-human," he is very human and truly fragile. He can preach the house down on Sunday morning, but be devastated by a low offering, low attendance, or what he perceives to be a bad sermon. This is when you need to be his greatest cheerleader, his biggest fan. Sometimes, just a simple, "Baby, I'm with you, and we will make it—together," can raise your husband's spirits and give him a renewed sense of hope.

    Without a doubt, Randy is my greatest cheerleader. So many times, he goes out of his way to encourage and edify me. He tells me I look good, even when I don't. He finds ways to coddle and pamper me (even if I don't deserve it!) and does things for me I would never do for myself. At times, it seems a bit overboard; but I have to admit, *I love it!* One thing he has discovered is how much I really enjoy a professional massage. So now, whenever I have a birthday, or for Christmas or special celebrations, I can count on one gift for sure—a gift certificate from my husband for a massage. Okay, it's a bit predictable, but who's complaining? I get to enjoy something I love from someone who loves me. Even when we go out of town, he always encourages me to take advantage of the spa amenities which are offered. You've got to love it!

In the same manner, many times I am Randy's greatest cheerleader and encourager. I find things he enjoys and make those things available to him. Actually, we have seen our marriage grow exponentially by just trying to out-serve and out-love one another. The more we love and serve each other, the more loving service we have to give to one another.

Put Your Best Foot Forward

True ministry does not "just happen." We all pray for it, plan for it, and put it in action. To be the best we can be and to be successful, requires a great amount of effort into our ministry lives. But the question remains: "Why do we not put as much

Because we are in the ministry, our marriages will be attacked on every level—spiritually, physically, emotionally, sexually, and financially.

effort into the success of our marriages? Why do we expect that our marriages will be successful simply because we are in the ministry?" The reality is that because we are in ministry, our marriages will be attacked on every level—spiritually, physically, emotionally, sexually, and financially. What have you done to withstand these assaults? What foundation have you built your marriage upon? Will you be prepared for inevitable difficult times, or will you just throw up your hands and walk away? Will you do the "right thing for the ministry" and put on a façade—your happy face—pretending everything is great? Or, will you work through the issue? The responsibility to make your marriage as healthy and successful as possible lies solely with you and your spouse. Successful marriages are developed using the same components as successful ministries: much prayer, planning, and action.

You are not only on the journey of a lifetime, but a lifetime journey, as well. You may be at the beginning or at a rest stop fueling up and gaining sustenance. Maybe you're at the halfway mark or

Successful marriages are developed using the same components as successful ministries: much prayer, planning, and action. You are not only on the journey of a lifetime, but a lifetime journey, as well.

close to the end of your journey? Regardless of your position or progress, begin today—right now—to make your marriage the best God intended it to be. Pray, plan, and act. Put forth your best effort and your best foot forward in order to make the journey the best it can be!

Being called by God to journey into ministry is such a privilege; how much more an honor to live this journey with the spouse whom God has given you!

Footnote:

"The only thing that children wear out faster than their
shoes is their parents."

John J. Plomp

7

Bronzed Shoes

My Issue: *Raising Preacher's Kids*

For many years, I have visited this couple who had the oddest decorations in their family room: a pair of bronzed baby shoes. I never fully understood where this idea came from, and the whole concept puzzled me. Still, being the good guest, I would always comment, "Oh, aren't they cute? How sweet! Whose shoes are these?" All the time I would be thinking to myself thoughts like, "How in the world could you fit your baby's feet into those? Wouldn't it hurt? How could they walk in them? Why have I never seen these in a shoe store?" Finally, a wise mother shared the bronze shoe secret with me. She said, "Jelly, these shoes weren't bronzed until the baby outgrew them! Now, they are a significant, treasured memory." Now I get it! Thankfully, they didn't have to wear these God-awful things in public! Needless to say, I was sorely relieved.

The significance of the bronzed baby shoes never fully made sense to me . . . until I, too, became a mother. As a mom,

I Have Issues

I tried to get booties to stay on my children's feet, but it didn't work. Neither did socks. As soon as I got them on the baby, Baby would pull them off. When Baby graduated to hard-soled shoes, I discovered the long-lost secret of keeping shoes on their feet: you must tie them up above their ankles and double knot the laces. This way, they would not come off Baby until I took them off. (Funny how their feet don't stink, isn't it? There is just something precious about baby's feet.)

Hard-soled shoes sent one, primary message to me: Baby is already growing up! In my mind, I could already see them walking across the stage to receive their high school diploma, so I knew I had to cherish the time we had together. Knowing I could never re-capture or re-live those special moments, I did the next best thing to make memories with my children by saving their baby clothes, baby blankets—and, yes, even their baby shoes. (Does anybody know where I can get three pairs of baby shoes bronzed?)

When I began to outline this chapter in my head, I decided to write a section on "What I Didn't Know Before I Became a Mother in Ministry" and another section on "What I Have Learned Since Becoming A Mother in Ministry." Then I realized the two could not be separated. Before motherhood, I knew absolutely nothing. (Truthfully, sometimes I still wonder if I know anything at all!) The things I've learned have only been because of constant interaction with my children and their friends. (The word "interaction" is used very loosely here! There are other words that could easily be used.) Now, as they grow toward adulthood at a seemingly record pace, I continue to learn. I am truly looking forward to the day my children see me as the Proverbs 31 woman and rise up and call me "blessed." Actually, this will probably not happen until they are grown and finally leave home. It is then when I will possibly seem smart and maybe a little wiser in their eyes. However, I am not holding my breath . . . I could die in the process! Maybe by their adulthood, I will have a little insight as to why I do the things I do, and they do the things they do. Until I arrive at that point in my life; hopefully, I can impart some understanding to help you in your journey.

The Life of a "P.K."

There is an old, African proverb which says, "It takes a village to raise a child," which implies that it does take more than one person to bring a child to mature adulthood. The development of your children really depends on many aspects too numerous to mention. Among those things would be the amount and the quality of time you have poured into their lives, how much you lived and demonstrated Jesus in front of them, if you heaped God's Word into their spirits, what they saw on television, the music they listened to, their friends, relatives, and how they were treated by people in

One of the largest influences on any preacher's kid: did you truly believe and live what you preached?

the church, just to name a few. Of all of these, one of the largest influences on any preacher's kid (better known as a "P.K.") stands out above the rest: did you and your husband, as their parents, truly believe and live what you preached? Believe me, kids are watching and listening—even at an earlier age than you would expect.

As the daughter of a minister, I learned first-hand what people in the church expect of their pastors' children. Some of their expectations were logical; others were totally unreasonable by anyone's standards. A few members seemed to draw their expectations straight from the pit of hell, as they were strictly designed to frustrate even the most perfect children in ministry, along with their parents. Living in my parent's fishbowl, I knew the pressures that well-meaning people could place on a P.K. Looking back on those years, there are many things I appreciate about my parents. But the one thing that stands out to me is they raised me and my sisters to be a *Christian*, not just a P.K. They lived throughout the week what they preached on Sundays. Never did I question why daddy said one thing on Sunday morning, but did not follow through with his words during the weekdays. My parents' greatest testimony is not that they pastored a great church, but that they raised three daughters who have all followed Christ in their adulthood. Now, those three daughters and their husbands are giving the same heritage to their own children.

Your children—just like your husband—are yours. Regardless of your position in the church or the community, you must place more emphasis on what *you* expect out of your children rather than what the *church* expects from them. As an adult P.K. and now a P. W. (Pastor's Wife), I do things because I am a Christian, not because I'm in the ministry. This is a life trait I learned from my parents; and now, my children are gleaning the same wisdom.

It may take an entire culture to raise a child, but it takes Godly parents to raise Godly children.

> *"Even the sparrow finds a home there, and the swallow builds her nest and raises her young—at a place near your altar, O Lord Almighty, my King and my God!"*

PSALM 84:3 (NLT)

Ministry Motherhood

I can never remember hearing anyone say that having children would be a picnic. In fact, the most advice I can remember hearing came from people telling me how my life would be completely changed once I had a child. There were those who would talk about children being the greatest joy one could ever experience, and my heart would leap with excitement. Then, there were those "prophets of doom" who felt their call in life was to tell me every P.K. horror story they had ever heard! "You know, those preacher's kids are always the worst ones," they would herald from the rooftops. I would respectfully listen, showing outward signs of agreement with the occasional nod, but I had the assurance in my heart that MY children would never cause me grief—especially since I would love them so much! I was convinced (just like every other mother I knew) that no one would ever love their kids as much as I would love mine. It just couldn't be possible. We would have a perfect life, in the perfect home, with the perfect church, and live in the perfect spiritual bubble so no sin would ever even think of entering their lives. And then . . . I woke up from my dream!

I Have Issues

After giving birth to my first child, my life was immediately infused with the necessity of being flexible and a certain knowing to always expect the unexpected. By the time my second and third child arrived, any and all plans had gone out the window and my flexibility had become a rubber band. Who could ever predict that the beautiful, new dress I had intended to wear on Sunday morning could either be covered at the top by baby barf, or in my lap by baby poop—and all before I even got out the front door. The clothes I had intended our children to wear on the same Sunday would be changed at least twice due to a various sundry of reasons. Play shoes (which were not the accepted church apparel) would sometimes be worn due to one dress shoe ending up in the toilet or simply lost forever. Of course, then I was expected to smile and be the "happy, happy pastor's wife" when I walked in the front door of the church. For some reason, people who had good noses didn't stay around long after getting a whiff of what my morning had already been like!

Then, there was lunch after the service which needed to be planned before we left for church. The menu usually had to be altered several times each morning because in the chaos of changing all of our clothes, I forgot to turn off the oven, and everything was burned to a crisp! During these moments of frustration, I found out the hard way that "anything you say can be used against you," and usually at the most inopportune time. I never expected these things to surface, so prior planning was never an issue up until this time. Somehow, in all of this chaos, God's divine plan for my life began a total metamorphosis.

Welcome to ministry motherhood.

Six P's for Raising P.K.s

*V*olumes of books could be written concerning the challenges and aspects of raising children in a ministry environment. Even though I do not claim to be the expert, I believe these are some of the most important and pressing issues concerning raising a P.K.

PERFECTION

Here is a derivative of the dreaded, seven-letter word: *perfect.* Just as the "perfect pastor's wife" is a myth, so are perfect pastor's kids. I can hear it now, "Well, you just haven't met MY perfect little angel!" Okay, maybe you think your little Johnny or Susie is a reincarnation of Jesus or Mother Mary, but those around you might say Lucifer or Beelzebub would be a closer comparison! Notice something which bears repeating: there is no perfect P.K. or perfect parent. This includes you and me, so go ahead and take off the "Supermom" cape!

I have watched so many ministry parents try everything under the sun to raise the perfect child. They read enough books to fill an entire library (and I do think you should read good, Godly books on child-rearing). They researched the Internet, tried to secure a proper balance of play time and work time, kept their kids in homeschool, and made all the right choices—at the right time—for their kids, all in the valiant effort of raising perfection. There is a Greek word for this effort: Ha! None of us live in a Utopian society and the sooner you realize there is no such thing as perfection in this life, the better you—and everyone around you—will be.

When our oldest daughter, Jordan, was in first grade she got into trouble at school one day. Her teacher was a minister's wife in a local church. When Mrs. Brown (the name has been changed to protect the guilty) called my husband into the classroom, she explained the problem Jordan was facing and her strategy to deal with it. She further expressed her concern as she knew how we would feel about Jordan's "problem." Finally, Mrs. Brown took the liberty to tell Jordan how she was supposed to be an example for the rest of the class, and that her continued misbehavior would be an embarrassment to her parents (us) and the big church her dad pastored. Unfortunately for Mrs. Brown, she did not know how *we* dealt with these types of issues.

Yes, we wanted Jordan to behave properly, but it had nothing to do with the fact that she was a P.K., or the possibility she would be an embarrassment to us or the church. We wanted good behavior because it was the *right* thing to do—period! Our lesson to her—and to Mrs. Brown—was: the certain way someone behaves, responds, or reacts is because of *who* they are, not *what* they are.

* *

The certain way someone behaves, responds, or reacts is because of who they are, not what they are.

* *

Somewhere down the line, your kids need to know they are not perfect, you are not perfect, and the people in your church are not perfect. Perfection is not the goal, because it is unobtainable;

however, *obedience* is what God expects from His children. Lead your kids to be Christ-like and not someone's ideal of perfection. There was a bumper sticker which read, "I'm not perfect, just forgiven." Always keep this in mind as you raise your children. Only in Heaven will perfection be attained, and this world, my friend, is a far cry from Heaven.

PERCEPTION

P.K.s are often given unrealistic expectations to live up to, and it's not fair to them or their parents. The last time I checked, I was not Mary, my husband wasn't Joseph, nor were our children part of the immaculate conception—and neither were yours! It has always puzzled me why minister's kids are supposed to grow up without any flaws, yet medical doctor's children can be sick and no one think a thing about it! You never hear of the school calling the plumber's kid to come fix the toilets, nor will you ever find a lawyer's child kept on a retainer to plead cases. Now, in no way am I saying minister's children should run wild and live like the devil, but there needs to be an understanding that just because they adorn the life of a P.K. does not make them alienated from the same temptations every child must learn to live through. Besides, they did not choose the role they have been asked to play. They were born into it.

Here is a major newsflash: just because you are in the ministry does not mean your child will be without sin. As parents, don't put those expectations on them or, better yet, never allow anyone else to do so either. While rearing a P.K. has its own, unique challenges, it is not totally different from raising any other children—with the exception of improbable expectations which again, are not realistic.

· ·

Newsflash: just because you are in the ministry does not mean your child will be without sin.

· ·

PERFORMANCE

This is the cousin to "perception." When people perceive your child to be something or someone, they always expect the accompanying performance as well. Again, this is unfair to your child and to you as the leader of the congregation. People will voice their request in questions like:

* "Why isn't your daughter involved in the drama team?"

* "My son is in the youth worship band and comes to practices on off-nights. Why isn't your son involved? After all, he is the pastor's kid and should be leading by example."

Well, maybe your son is not musically inclined or your daughter is a bad actress or shy in front of people. Maybe their talents and gifting are in other areas such as audio/video or caring for the elderly.

One of the worst things I believe any ministry parent can do is to force their child into something strictly to appease the expectations of the congregation. The antidote is to give your child choices and options. Something like, "Mark, you really can sing. How about joining the youth worship band? That would be a great outlet for your gift," will go much farther than, "Mark, you are the pastor's son, and it looks bad when you are not involved in the youth worship team. So, get up and get to rehearsal."

To ask a child, or a teenager for that matter, to be on the same spiritual level as an adult is another "performance" expectation which is unfair. As they grow and mature naturally, they are also growing and maturing spiritually as well. To ask your 13 year-old to fast from food for 30 days is neither practical nor healthy. Thirteen year-olds need to eat—and eat a lot! Maybe they can fast other items such as television or video games for 30 days and devote that time to God by serving others or working in the church. Again, the key is to help your child find their own place in God so they can feel a sense of accomplishment by doing what is in their heart to do. Not only will this release a great sense of fulfillment, it will also teach them to not be man-pleasers with eye service only, but to please God with their heart devoted to Him and His work.

PRESSURE

Let's face it. Every child/teenager is faced with enormous pressure in today's world. I sometimes cringe at the things I hear my kids tell me they heard at school, around classmates, or can be overheard in conversation. Kids have enough to deal with, without the added pressure of being a P.K.; however, the pressure to perform goes with the territory in most ministry families.

Pressure to perform can come from various places. It can be imposed by parishioners, parentally, or it can be self-imposed. If your child is feeling this type of pressure, as a parent, you should be able to correctly assess where the pressure is coming from and why it is there. Pressure from parishioners should come only with the approval of the parents. Pressure from parents comes with every walk of life and must be assessed with each situation. Self-imposed pressure is the most difficult because you, as a parent, cannot control the parameter of this type of pressure to perform.

When our middle daughter, Danielle, was in middle school, she did not want to be in the children's choir any longer. She was in that "tweener" group—you know, too old for children's church, too young for youth group—and was unhappy with being involved with the younger kids. I knew the oldest children in the choir were the most capable for the lead parts, so I thought she would enjoy playing a lead in the summer play. I basically forced her to do it, and she hated it! To this day, I can still hear her saying, "Mom, this is so lame." Her attitude was bad and her performance would have reflected it; however, I knew if she quit, other children her age would follow. As her parent, I began to quickly realize a few important things:

* She was a leader and would lead in attitude, good or bad.

* Others would follow her regardless of what I made her do. This was out of my control.

* She had grown up much faster than I had thought.

* It just wasn't worth the fight. (Important lesson here: learn to pick your battles!)

* I could relieve some of her performance pressure if I chose.

So, we had a talk and came to a compromise that if she would complete the summer play, it would be her last. I asked her to do her best, to excel in every aspect including her attitude, and wear a happy face while doing it. She agreed to our terms and in the end, she was marvelous at her leading role and enjoyed doing it. Staying true to our agreement, she did not do another one! When she quit performing, other children did follow her, but not as many as I had feared would do so.

Whether it is participating in a children's play or having to hear parishioners complain about "those short dresses the pastor's daughter wears," pressure from being a P.K. is eminent. Your job, as their parent, is to be the balance between what is unrealistic pressure and what God's Word says concerning the issues. In the end, only the Word of God will be the measuring stick as to what is truly acceptable and what is man-made pressure.

PRAYER

First, I should assume that you actually do pray for your children, husband, and family. If you don't then start . . . and start *now*! Many minister's wives think their position replaces their personal responsibility, but it doesn't. Prayer should be an integral part of your daily life, especially when you are parent. You should find yourself praying at odd times of the day, talking to Jesus when no one else is around, and developing a nature to pray if you only have just a moment to reflect. I believe the verse Paul wrote to "Pray without ceasing" was written with mothers in mind, especially for those who are in the ministry and have children.[1]

Just as the seasons of life change, so do the prayers of a righteous mother. As an expectant mother, you probably found

---

1 See 1 Thessalonians 5:17

yourself praying for a healthy and whole child—one with all ten fingers and toes—a quick labor and delivery, and the wisdom to be a good mother. It is always good to pray for a healthy child and wisdom, but specific prayer focuses will definitely change as your child goes through the stages of life.

For example, when my children were babies, I would ask God to help me be a positive, Godly influence in their lives. But, as they grew older, my prayer focus began to change, as now, they were being an influence on people, and other people were influencing their lives as well. Over the years, I have made many additions to my prayer list concerning my children including their friends, teachers, grades, bus drivers, lunch room ladies, coaches, driver's education teacher (They got a lot of prayer!), new bosses, future spouses, and many more. Some things remained constant like praying for their hunger for the things of God, the call of God on their lives, preparation for the workforce and ministry, etcetera.

One thing never changes: parenting never gets easier. It does, however, never cease to change. Be prepared to adjust and roll with the changes. It's a fun and challenging ride!

You might be the pastor to the congregation, but you are a parent to your children.

PREPARATION

It seems that many ministers are so focused on preparing their congregations and staffs, that they overlook the most important people in which they are personally called to develop—their own children. A good rule to keep close to your heart is this: you might be the *pastor* to the congregation, but you are a *parent* to your children. Too many ministers try and mix the two, and it never works. The difference is the distinction between training and instructing.

· ·

The key ingredient to training is simple—time!

· ·

To "train" a child is a whole different world than "instructing" a child. Most parents think their instructions serve the purpose of training. Sadly, they do not. Instructions are told or laid out, while training is the proper implementation of instructions. When you go to the gym and need some assistance in your workout routine, you never ask for a personal "instructor." No, you secure the services of a personal "trainer." Why? Because you probably already know the instructions for losing weight, but you need someone to walk you through the program. Championship boxers have trainers, not instructors. Even dogs can understand some verbal commands, but a pet trainer can change the behavior of an animal seemingly overnight. In the same manner, "training a child" includes helping him/her understand who they are, where they are gifted, where they are challenged, and what they can do in life outside of just religious matters. The key ingredient to training is simple—TIME! There can be no training—whether it be a child, a boxer, or an animal—without an investment of time.

At one point in life, I had greatly mistaken the idea that training a child according to the book of Proverbs meant your child would never experience any difficulties in their desire to follow Christ. Again, another wrong assumption. I could not rationalize how good parents with good marriages and strong family values sometimes had children who strayed away from God. Some of those children had been in church and around the things of God their entire lives. Then, the same thing happened to my children as they began to get older. This only added to my confusion as I knew first-hand how Randy and I lived our lives both privately and with our children. As I began to question the Father, I came up with some simple, yet profound, answers which began to help me.

Training a child *"in the way he should go"* [2] encompasses more than just religious training. It deals with issues like developing personality types. For instance, you cannot make an introvert child live like an extrovert. It includes finding their potential, navigating them to find their niche and passion in life, and much more. I found by taking this premise, it allowed me to strengthen them with their vocation in life and their future spouse and family, along with their relationship with God. After all, who am I to think my strength and training could be greater than God's? The greatest truth I realized was that my child's eternity is *not* based on me, but rather on how *they* respond to God and the harvest *they* reap from seeds *they* have planted. As a parent, our job is to point our children in the right direction and pray for God's grace and mercy to be in action.

---

2 See Proverbs 22:6

Even though I could not see my daughter or know her thoughts, I came to realize I served a God who did know everything about her and cared for her more than I ever could. Trusting in God during this situation did pay off. She came home, restored her relationship with God, and as I am writing this book, is a now a minister of the Gospel of Jesus Christ!

Love the Bronzed Shoes

Once upon a time, I was slightly forgetful. Even though I have forgotten many smaller things in life, I can honestly say I have never forgotten one of my children. Randy on the other hand . . . well, that's a different story altogether!

When I was pregnant with our youngest daughter, Alayna, Randy and I had risen to an economic level which allowed us to have two cars, thus giving us the opportunity to travel to and from the church separately. After church one evening, I was particularly tired and needed to go straight home after the service concluded. I asked Randy to retrieve our sleeping six year-old, Danielle, from the front pew. "Sure, Dear, that will be no problem," he assured me. But he got distracted . . . and you know the rest of the story. Randy locked up the church, came home, and started to relax when I realized Danielle was not with him. (If you're laughing now, more than likely, this has happened to you in some fashion.) He quickly returned to the church and found her on the front pew. All the lights were out, everyone else had gone home, and she was the only one still in the auditorium. Danielle was still sound asleep and never was awakened to be frightened. I cannot say the same for Randy or myself.

This story reveals something more important than to never leave your sleeping child at church for your husband to bring home! It is a clear reminder that, truly, the most important physical thing in your ministry is your family. Anyone else can turn the lights out, leave the church, and go home. You can even leave the city where you currently serve and move to another pastorate, but you will still have your family. Love them unconditionally, without reservation, and without end. When everything and everyone else is gone, they are all that is truly important and valuable!

Footnote:

"Is it time to go home yet? I keep clicking my heels . . ."

8

House Shoes

MY ISSUE: *MY HOUSE, MY HOME*

*G*ranny Talbert was a wonderful woman. She was extremely stubborn but had a really good heart. There were certain things
Granny did that you always could expect: she always had candy on
her end table, she smelled like Chantilly® or White Shoulders®, she
hid her money in her brassiere, and she wore Daniel Greene house
shoes. It never really occurred to Granny that there were any other
companies who designed house shoes, but it wouldn't have made any
difference. As far as she was concerned, it was Daniel Greene house
shoes or nothing else. Whenever Granny Talbert went to buy a pair
of Daniel Greene house shoes and they were out of her size, she went
on a mission to find them somewhere else (or at least she directed the
store personnel to do so). When they couldn't find them, I can still
hear her say, "Well, pfsht!"

Granny had really tiny feet. I was about ten years old; and
whenever I would go to visit her, I immediately found myself in her

closet looking for a pair of house shoes that I would wear for the remainder of my visit. They did not even look like house shoes to me. Some had tiny heels, others had had high heels and feathers. Some were shiny and made from a fabric which looked a little like brocade. Some were damask. There were loafers, mules, and fluffy slides. As soon as a new style was released, Granny would hurry out and buy them. I never really figured out what was so special about those Daniel Greene shoes she wore, but as soon as she got home, she would immediately slip into a pair.

At about ten and a half, I couldn't wear them any longer. Those were some of the best six months of my life because those were the fanciest shoes I can ever remember wearing as a child.

Although Granny could not walk very well in her last days, she always kept a pair of Daniel Greene slippers by her bed, just in case she needed them. The last time I was able to converse with her, she was in the hospital in Nashville. I bent over her bed to kiss her, and she said, "Careful, Jelly, don't step on my house shoes." She died about three days later and was buried in a white nurse's uniform and—you guessed it—a pair of her favorite Daniel Greene house shoes! I guess she wanted to be really at home in Heaven.

Your House, Your Home

*I*t was not hard for me to get excited about setting up my own home after Randy and I decided to get married. I had a hope chest for years, so there was very little we really needed to purchase. I had most of the linens, kitchen items, and décor items. Plus, my parents gave us a bedroom suite, and Randy's parents gave us $400.00 to buy whatever else we needed. We paid our tithes, then bought a couch, loveseat, chair, ottoman, recliner, coffee table, two end tables, two lamps, a dinette table with four chairs, and a set of golf clubs—all with that $400.00! What a deal! During our first year, we focused on finishing school, working, and interning. We didn't make very much money, but we also didn't go into debt as we watched every dime by dining frugally and limiting our expenses.

Our little apartment stayed pretty clean that year, mainly because we were rarely at home. It was only after we got more stuff, a bigger place, a busier life, and children, that the challenges of cleanliness and order began to stalk us.

Through the years, I have developed some home principles which have saved me on numerous occasions. Again, I don't claim to be Martha Stewart, Rachel Ray, or Betty Crocker, but I have lived, not only with a husband and children, but also in the fishbowl of ministry. Hopefully, some of these things will be a help to you on your journey.

1. **Don't try to have it all now.** It is good to look forward to purchasing something, when you can really afford it. There is nothing wrong with saving for the future, learning to sacrifice and do without, and not going deeply into debt for things you may not even want five years from now—even if you think you just can't live without it now. This type of structure will also help your children begin learning the monetary principles of saving and avoiding instant gratification.

2. **Your home is just that—your home.** Enjoy it, and allow your family to enjoy it. If there are rooms you want to keep clean, then lock them, bar them, or put an alarm over

the threshold. It is not worth yelling at your family every time they have made a mess of your special room.

3. **Guard your home as your sanctuary.** If you need to have people over occasionally, do so, but don't allow it to interfere with all your family time. Being in the ministry, your children already feel as though they have to share their parents with everyone in the church; and to some degree, they are right. Protect your family and the time you have allotted to spend with them. There are times when we retreat to the family room in our basement. We turn off all of the lights and the ringers on the telephones (cell phones included!), close the garage doors, and pretend we are not at home. If the doorbell rings, we ignore it. Only an emergency can get us out of hiding.

   Don't allow unimportant interruptions to steal important moments from your children and your spouse. They will be grateful for the uninterrupted time you make and spend with them.

4. **Set boundaries for the people in your church.** This is especially true if you live in the church parsonage or close to the church. Help them understand that this is the place of your residence—your home—and not just a church parsonage or an extension of the church.

   Before we married, Randy was a part-time youth pastor at a little church in Florida, and the parsonage was next door to the church. On Sunday mornings, many of the church members would visit the pastor's home before services began. The parsonage soon became a first aid station, coffee house, donut shop, nursery, and a hosiery store! It was only after the pastor had a little chat with the church board that the members began to have more respect for his family privacy.

If you have to have one of these discussions with the board or members, there will be those who will breach the boundaries. It happens all the time, in different towns, with different faces. However, when a line is crossed, you must deal with it as needed. Sometimes a gentle admonition will stop the problem. At other times, sharper words are required. Just remember, not everyone has good social skills, and they truly might not understand they are violating private space. With these types, use the opportunity to mentor them in gentleness.

5. **Learn to separate "important" from "urgent."** Believe me, there is a difference. Suppose someone forgets to ask you, until the very last possible moment, to provide a homemade dessert for the ladies meeting the same night your son has a Little League game. Now, you must make a choice: to keep the ladies happy or watch your son play baseball. My advice? Go to the ballgame. Your attendance and support will be much more important to your child than a homemade dessert is to a bunch of women. (They probably don't need it anyway!)

Side note: remember that "homemade" does not always have to mean "from scratch!" Find some quick things you can throw together that looks like you slaved in the kitchen all day preparing it!

6. **Find a productive way to alleviate stress.** Stress is inevitable no matter who you are, where you live, or how much money you have or don't have. If you are angry, scrub the bath tub, mow the yard, or throw rocks into the ditch. If you are sad, put on some happy music and mop your floors. Whenever I get under stress, I go to the kitchen and begin to cook. My family loves my stress relief! It depends on the amount of stress I am experiencing as to how long I will cook. I may prepare meals for two or three days at a time or desserts for an entire holiday season.

7. **Be creative when possible.** Don't let your meals, your house, or your love life become routine. Find ways to do things differently. Read cookbooks and time-saving tips on making great family dinners. Search the Internet for ideas on how to organize your life and improve your family life. Watch home decorating programs for new ideas on how to spruce up your home. (Believe me, the "do it yourself" ideas can turn anyone into a decorating genius!) Make plans with your husband to attend a marriage seminar—outside the church, if necessary—to add creative and fun ways to strengthen your marriage and intimacy. The key element here: keep it fresh! Stay interested and interesting.

8. **Remember God is a God of order.** Do you ever feel as though your entire world is in one massive layer of chaos? We all have. When things seem out of control, remember God is always in control. Take a look at creation, and the way He created life in a certain order. What would He have done with the land animals if they were created before any

*When things seem out of control,
remember God is always in control.*

land to inhabit? There is hope for you to put your home and life in order. If you cannot get ahead of the clutter, get rid of the clutter. If you cannot find time to do what is necessary, then super-organize your day by making a list of things to do in order of priority. Then, spend *only* the allotted time for each task and cross out each thing when it's completed. (There's something very encouraging about seeing a "to do" list with things crossed out!) Be realistic with the amount of time it takes to complete the task. Only do one huge project each week.

A friend of mine, wanting to simplify her life, decided she was going to wear only black, tan, white, and navy clothing. This would have never worked in a million years for me, but it proved to be a major time-saver for her and gave her a huge sense of organization. She never had to lose time worrying about what she was going to wear. With this new system, everything always matched.

9. **Simplify your home as much as possible.** My mother use to say, "Have a place for everything and put everything in its place." That sounded really useless while I was a

teenager; but now, it is the gospel at our house!

In our home, everyone has their own bedroom, except Randy. He and I share the same room. (smiles!) Anyways, the rule in our home is: "take it to your room when you come in." Shoes, book bags, mail, earrings, etcetera—it all goes to the owner's bedroom. If I find stuff in the wrong place, I either hide it or hold it for ransom. Ransom usually consists of washing dishes after dinner or vacuuming the floors. Hiding it is a lot of fun for me, especially when I get to say, "No, you're cold, freezing, warmer, hot, HOT, BURNING UP!" Either way, the message comes across clear: put things where they belong.

10. **Be flexible.** Being in the ministry, you will always have unexpected guests, like the board members' family who wants to come and have dinner, as well as a slew of unplanned activities. Be flexible and operate in a spirit of graciousness and hospitality. Just put another potato in the pot or pull out the left-over food from last night. Unexpected guests should not be offended by left-overs. If they are, gently remind them they were unexpected!

I am married to "Mr. Impromptu," and he has successfully raised our three children to be just like him. Over the years, I have frequently found myself to be the hostess for an after church party, a football game party, or a car washing party, all with little-to-no warning. Of course, this does not account for the phone calls I overheard which said, "Do you want to come over tonight? Mom's cooking!" One of our daughters, Danielle, had her friends over so often at dinner, the neighbors thought we had adopted another child.

Being flexible does not come natural for me and has been a hard lesson to learn. Mr. Impromptu and his children have required that I learn to bend. At times, I have felt like a pretzel, at other times a rubber band, and on a few severe occasions, you could have called me Gumby! All in all, I have learned so much from those who have been in our home, plus my family has been entertained and happy. This new dimension added to my life has been for the good . . . at least, most of the time.

One major lesson I have learned: your attitude while working through the unexpected guest or function is paramount to the outcome. Whenever I do have the unexpected, I just make it work with what I have. After the entertainment, I leave the clean-up to the person who planned the party or decided to just show up! I have never had a complaint. They are just happy to eat.

Footnote:

"If I have learned one thing in this life, it is that God will
not tie my shoes without me."

Doug Boyd

9

Re-Soled

My Issue: *Comfort and Retreat*

Every woman has at least one pair of truly comfortable shoes. When we have had a rough day and need to relax, we supernaturally gravitate to these shoes every time. Some of my favorite, most comfortable shoes are my bedroom slippers, especially those which match my p.j.'s. (Geez, I sound like my grandmother!) In fact, I probably have six or seven pair of bedroom slippers, all with real soles on the bottoms to protect my feet in the event I need to go outside. My favorite style are the black felt ones with the flexible, rubber sole. They also have a toggle on the top so I could loosen or tighten the slipper, depending if my feet were swollen at the moment or not.

One day, much to my dismay, my favorite slippers disappeared! Nobody took them. No one had seen them. I looked in the bedroom, the closet, the laundry room, the basement, outside, under the bed, everywhere someone could think of to look. I went through my most recently-used suitcases to see if I had forgotten to unpack them. I even looked in the dog's kennel and his favorite hiding place to see if he had possibly taken them. No such luck. The slippers could not be found. I must have had a "pre-senior" moment and taken them off, only to forget where they were hiding. It wasn't the fact that I didn't have any others to wear; I just hate to lose anything, especially my favorite, comfortable shoes. Coming to the realization that my slippers were gone for good, I began to look for a replacement pair, without much success.

None of my children wear the same size shoe as me. All of my girls have longer feet, and they usually don't even like my style—thank goodness! One day, while taking our youngest daughter to school, I noticed something on her feet which looked vaguely familiar. I pulled up her pants leg and then became even more confused. Funny, I remember having a pair of bedroom slippers that were very similar to her school shoes. M–m-m-m . . .

Alayna looked at me very sheepishly when I asked her, "So, when and where did we get these?" I was truly asking so I could get a pair for me, seeing as they would work as bedroom slippers. Then, it dawned on me like a ton of bricks. "Hey! These aren't her school moccasins! They are my missing slippers that were worn out and filthy!" All of the time I had spent looking for these, and the whole time they were on her feet! She had found my most comfortable pair of shoes, secretly confiscated them, and had stretched them out so much, no amount of adjusting that toggle would ever make them fit my feet again. Her reasoning was, "Mom, they are only bedroom slippers. Relax. You can get some more."

She just did not understand. They were not just "bedroom slippers," but rather, my *favorite* relaxing shoes. When I wore them, my feet felt good. When my feet feel good, my whole body feels good. Just looking at those shoes made me start to mentally rest, relax, and renew myself. Without those shoes, how would I ever know when to relax? Oh, the struggles we face!

Remember the Sabbath, Superman!

I don't know where we have gotten the idea that we are supposed to be indestructible, but this thought has somehow pervaded the lives of those in ministry. Satan has tricked us into thinking we are above any kind of physical or mental failure, using the "lack of faith" weapon as his chief, manipulative tool. The painful reality is that ministers are not exempt from experiencing physical and mental failure. It is brought before our eyes each time we see it demonstrated in one of our fallen spiritual heroes. The idea which says we—ourselves or those we hold in high esteem—are invincible is severely dangerous. Satan's other chief weapon is to keep us so busy concerning the business of the church and the Kingdom, that we don't take the time off to rest and renew our own spirits and minds. Our busy-ness is not a sign of our righteousness or Godliness.

Our busy-ness is not a sign of our righteousness or Godliness.

God gave Man a plan to follow when He created the heavens and the earth in that He rested on the seventh day. He even made rest a commandment:

"Remember the sabbath day, to keep it holy."

EXODUS 20:8

God created us. He knows our limitations. He knows the importance of rest. So, why do we think rest is unnecessary and even a sign of laziness? We make the mistake of thinking since we are working for the Lord, then rest is unnecessary or unspiritual. In our minds, we have followed the commandments of God since we are in church every Sunday and sometimes several times throughout the week. That's all the rest we need, right? Wrong!

God did not command us to go to church on Sunday. He did not say teach a Sunday School class, sing in the choir, make the announcements, and then entertain a dozen people over for Sunday lunch. Even though these things are important in the Kingdom of God and constitute "keeping the Sabbath holy," they can never be counted as "rest." Rest is whatever brings you new energy to continue in your work for the Lord. Just like any other minister, Sunday is never a "rest" day in our home; however, it is also not a shopping day, a laundry day, or a party day. Because of our numerous functions and duties on that day, we do not physically or mentally rest, but we do honor the day with somewhat limited activity.

I am not saying we, as ministers, should stop having church or attending church functions; that would be ludicrous. What I believe needs to be seen is the fact that ministers and their families need to find activities to refresh themselves. We must find some time to rest and honor the Sabbath, which is not a day of the week, but a principle behind the commandment. Maybe your "Sabbath" might be a Tuesday or Monday or Friday. Whichever one works, establish a dedicated "Sabbath" for rest and renewal. If you aren't refreshed, you are only going to give out stale food, and not the Bread of Life, to those you serve.

The Three "R's"

*A*uthor Rick Warren tells us we should divert daily, withdraw weekly, and abandon annually.[1] This is some of the best advice I have ever read, especially as it pertains to the life of a minister and their family. I relate daily diversion to relaxation, weekly withdrawal to rest, and annual abandonment to rejuvenation. Each play a vital part to our physical, emotional, and spiritual health and carry very distinguishable differences.

1. **Relaxation** is taking some time to go to a movie or having dinner out. (Anytime I do not have to cook is a banner day for me!) My husband relaxes on the golf course, but he doesn't necessarily rest. Just putting your feet up on the end of the sofa and enjoying a cup of coffee for a few moments may bring a sense of relaxation. I find it very relaxing to pet my dog. However, as I said earlier, none of these things truly constitute keeping the Sabbath holy.

2. **Rest** comes when your body and mind take a pit-stop for refueling. This may come by reading a book or going away for a day trip with nothing planned. Relaxation must precede rest; if it doesn't, you will feel more tired than when you

---

1 Christian Post, Guest Columnist, *"The Seven Foundations of Jesus Leadership,"* April 23, 2008.

Rejuvenation is getting away to receive something.

began your "time of rest." Think about how many times you have come back from a vacation only to say, "I need a vacation to rest from my vacation!" This is what happens when relaxation does not happen before rest.

3. **Rejuvenation** is when you receive the nutrition necessary for your spirit to go the next level. It's more than just "getting away" from something; it is getting away to receive something. Rejuvenation comes only after you have relaxed your mind, rested your body, and fed your spirit.

Some great scriptures concerning the value of relaxation, rest, and rejuvenation are:

"For which cause we faint not; but though our outward man perish, yet the inward man is renewed day by day."

2 CORINTHIANS 4:16 (KJV)

"And I said, Oh that I had wings like a dove! for then would I fly away, and be at rest. Lo, then would I wander far off, and remain in the wilderness. Selah. I would

hasten my escape from the windy storm and tempest."

PSALMS 55:6-8 (KJV)

I can vividly remember times in my own life when I felt like I never wanted to go to church again. I never wanted to help another person, never wanted to pick up another baby, never wanted to pseudo-smile at anyone again. It was then I realized the frailty of my own strength, and I desperately needed a retreat or, at least, a little time away. That moment usually came at the most inopportune time, when it was never convenient to get away. But I had to ask myself, "When is it 'convenient' to have a nervous breakdown?" If you are like I was and truly at the very end of your proverbial rope, you'd better either get away quickly or find a way to relieve the stressors in your life. Your life, ministry, family, and effectiveness to others will depend on it.

I had to ask myself, "When is it 'convenient' to have a nervous break-down?"

Stress Relievers

1. **Plan some time to get away and anticipate it.** It may only be a lunch hour or a get-away day, week, or month. Just plan it.

It will never happen by accident and rarely on the spur of the moment. We all need a break. The government even recognizes that employees need to take a few minutes every so often to refresh themselves; thus, they require all employers to have mandatory "breaks" in their employees' daily work routines. Sometimes the break might consist of going to a certain room, having a little conversation, a drink, a bite of food, and a potty break. At times, just getting away from the telephone for a few minutes helps to refresh the mind. One of our administrative assistants finds an empty stairwell to sit in and has her lunch break with a book. She always comes back refreshed.

I have a very restful "prayer closet." It is in my bedroom—on my side of the bed! When everyone in our house has gone and are fulfilling their daily duties, I utilize this space by going back to bed. I used to feel so guilty about doing this until I realized how much better I felt after spending a little more time there. After I re-named my side of the bed my "Prayer Closet," I found it easier to explain my activity to anyone who called and asked what I was doing. "I'm in my prayer closet." Often, I do pray and meditate there. I find more prayer happens for me when I am horizontal.

It is not always possible to take a week off or even a day off, but we can separate ourselves for a few moments. Find the thing which helps you to relax and find a way to do it when your stress level starts rising. Oh yeah, and don't be afraid that the ministry will stop if you aren't there. Remember, the ministry belongs to one God, and you're not Him!

2. **Take a leave of absence from some of your duties.** You don't have to do everything, all the time! Give someone else

an opportunity to serve—even if they cannot do it with your expertise. Give them the freedom to fail. How else will they learn? Think about it. How did you learn?

3. **Take a class on something not church-related.** Check out your local colleges, gyms, or recreational centers, just as long as they are not associated with the church. You will be amazed at how just seeing a different sect of people will help change your perspective.

4. **Learn deep breathing exercises.** It really does help.

5. **Count to one hundred and then do it backwards.** It really does help.

6. **Scream into a pillow for a short time or stomp your feet.** If you do decide to do this, be sure no one else is around! It isn't an example you would want your children or a church member to repeat frequently. At one time, I had a temper tantrum mat. When I needed to throw a fit, I would take my little mat to the closet and throw a good one. Of course, no one was looking!

7. **Get a job to help cut down on some of your volunteerism.** Even if it is only a part-time job. People have a tendency to ask less of you if they know you are employed outside of the church.

8. **Take up the offer from a church member for you and your husband to go on a mini-vacation.** Use it as a prayer retreat if need be.

9. **Take advantage of a time-share offer.** You know, the ones where you get three days/two nights at a resort to listen to them try to sell you a vacation plan. Once you tell them how much money you and your spouse make, they really will know you can't afford it! WARNING: Do not do this if you are easily swayed by the "deal of the century" and cannot say, "No!" This could cause more stress than you originally planned to get away from.

10. **Go on a picnic with your spouse.** It does not need to cost a lot of money. Just take a blanket, some food, a bottle of sparking grape juice, and have some time alone. Leave the cell phones in the car. Not only will you feel relaxed, but you will also help your spouse to feel cherished and relaxed.

11. **Take your kids, one of their friends, and one of their parents to a playground or a park.** While the kids play, you can have an adult conversation. That always goes a long way toward alleviating life's issues. It can also give you a fresh perspective on your problems.

12. **Re-arrange the furniture in the bedroom.** It may psyche you into thinking that you really are on a vacation when you wake up in a strange room! Sometimes, this little trick will go a long way in bringing down your stress level. You'd be amazed what a change of scenery can do for you!

13. **Refrain from sad chick-flicks!** Unless you are at the point that you need a good cry. If this is the case, go to the matinee

when no one else is there, and you can really wail in peace.

All of these things, and many others, are very simple stress relievers. The goal is to find something to relieve the stress in your life. There is no way to totally alleviate it, but you can find something to at least release the pressure valve. Even if it means only putting on a pair of bedroom slippers and telling yourself that it is time to relax, do it.

Footnote:

"Sometimes they just need to put on travelin' shoes!"

10

The Devil Wears Fake Prada

MY ISSUE: *WOMEN IN THE PEWS*

We all have an idea in our minds of what the devil looks like. Most of us have had the image, at some time or another, of a man in a red suit with pointed ears, a pitched-fork tail, hooves instead of feet, and horns on his head. If we could be assured this was exactly how the devil looked, then we would have no trouble identifying him when he came to cause havoc in our lives. Unfortunately, we have no assurance of appearance or features. According to the Bible, he can appear as an angel of light, a serpent, a roaring lion, Heaven's choir director, and even ascended as the dawn of the morning. He became filled with pride and thought he was important enough to fill God's shoes, which God took issue with by throwing him out of Heaven.

The devil may have many masquerades, but there is one thing he is and will always be—a deceiver. The Bible properly describes his nature as the *"father of lies."* [1] As Godly women, we have a responsibility to recognize and help our husbands recognize the wiles of Satan. Anyone can be deceived, even those who are devoting their lives daily to God's Word and His work.

This scenario is all too common with ministers (a.k.a. our husbands!): some woman from the church sees the load we are carrying and feels "called by God" to offer assistance and help relieve some of the burdens. They are quick to provide a needed hand, lighten the load, entertain us, and make themselves indispensable to the ministry. They hardly ever focus just on our husbands, as their motives would quickly be uncovered. Eventually, though, the other shoe drops, and the real issue is exposed. Their agenda is not to help and to be a "blessing" but rather to seduce our husbands and sabotage the ministry. If only they had cloven hooves and had adorned themselves in a red devil suit, we could have recognized the fake imitation. The deception and disloyalty would have been avoided. But that's never how it happens!

I can go to just about any place in Asia, and even some places in the United States and purchase "knock-off" brand-name shoes. They may look like Prada®, but they will never possess the same quality the designer originally intended. In the same manner, if Satan had taken God's place in Heaven, he would have been a false god—a counterfeit. Likewise, if someone tries to take your place in the life of your husband, that person will only be a "knock-off" and not the real thing. Just like fake shoes, they are merely a poor imitation of the real thing.

---

1 John 8:44

Protect This House

There is almost nothing as stimulating and exciting as a college football game. The student body, the fans, and the community support. Everything about the atmosphere breeds energy and excitement. Obviously, every team prepares to win every game, whether they are the underdogs or favorites. However, there is an innate pride and pressure to win on your own field. Today, many teams, as they move down through the tunnel from the locker room to the jam-packed, fan-crazed stadium, have a sign posted over the exit of the tunnel which reads, "We Must Protect This House!" It is the final charge to the home team to not let the visitor come onto their field and leave with a victory.

I think it would be a great idea for some minister's wives to place the same sign over their front door! Or better yet, over their bedroom door. God has given you a gift in your husband, and by nature, it is your innate responsibility to protect your house! This is a motto I have used since the day we were married and still remind myself of this responsibility daily.

I could fill another entire book with stories of women who have tried to come after my husband, totally convinced that they would be a better mate for him than I am. One word can describe these women: fools! Of course, in the same book, I could also tell how, in one particular incident, the Spirit of God warned me and my husband about how Satan was being used in the form of a woman.

If you do not remember anything else I write in this chapter, remember this: God has given you a spirit of discernment, and you are right! The Holy Spirit knows the heart and intentions of people; and if you will stay in tune with Him, He will give you the weapons to "Protect Your House!"

. . . .

God has given you a spirit of discernment, and you are right!

. . . .

Hands Off, Chick!

There was once a lady in our church who began to give little gifts to my husband. Those gifts started out small and inexpensive, but grew significantly larger and higher in value as time went on. Randy never thought a thing about what she was doing. In his eyes, she was just being kind; in my eyes, she was kind of devious! My suspicions of her motives grew when I realized she never included me in the gift giving or in the presentation of the gift to my husband. Honestly, I didn't need her little prizes *and neither did my husband!* After I warned Randy, he began to clue in on some of the little innuendoes she was making in conversation and started to steer clear of her. One day, she made the fatal mistake of telling someone else that Pastor Randy was wearing the tie and tie pin she had bought him. She thought she had some bragging rights—over a tie! Little did she know that I overheard her conversation! She found out very quickly that NO WOMAN has any rights over MY HUSBAND regardless of how many gifts she has bought. Mysteriously, all of her little gifts disappeared from the closet. She eventually got the message that neither she, nor her gifts, were welcomed and/or had any place in our closet or our lives.

Many years ago, there was another woman in our church who absolutely hated me. (Can you believe it? How can you not love me?!) In my opinion, she really had no reason to feel so strongly against me, but she did. Even though I was young and not very wise, I could sense a spirit of jealousy in her. I quickly realized that she wanted my husband to be her husband. At first, Randy thought I was crazy and was the one dealing with jealousy. But, he honored my feelings and established boundaries to protect himself from her. He did not counsel her in private, grant her private conversations, and included her husband when they would talk at church. A few years later, she made a blatant pass at him, thinking he would feel honored to know she felt that way about him. After he rejected her "pass," he immediately called and told me what had happened. Of course, I was able to say, "I told you so!" (But, I did say it gently!)

If Satan can destroy your home, he will destroy your ministry and the influence you have on an untold number of lives.

Over the years of our ministry, God has always given us warning signs—sometimes for me to warn Randy, and other times Randy has had to warn me. It is our responsibility to listen to the voice of God and respond when one of us is feeling uneasy. It is no secret that Satan is continuously looking for ways to destroy those

When God calls me to do something, it is not because I can, but because He wants me to find a new strength and develop it.

who are in the ministry. You and your husband basically have a big bull's eye placed on your marriage and your home. Why? Because if Satan can destroy your home, he will destroy your ministry and the influence you have on an untold number of lives. This is why we need to heed the voice of God and learn to be, as the Bible says, "wise as serpents."[2]

A woman's intuition, combined with the Spirit of God, is a pretty accurate reading when it comes to dealing with our husbands. However, there is a personal issue—actually a sin issue—in which no one likes to talk about that can severely cloud our judgment: the issue of jealousy. Jealousy is a sister to covetousness. Whenever those red flags come out spotting a "fake Prada®," make sure to check your own motives first. Sometimes, our own issues with jealousy and insecurity make us put up walls which are not necessary. I have actually known minister's wives who could not get a handle on their own jealousy, and eventually drove their husband to another woman who, at first, had no wrong intentions. Ask God for His wisdom and discernment concerning these issues and let Him work out any jealousy or envy which may

---

2   See Matthew 10:16

reside in your heart. Believe me, the counterfeits are easy to see when you are not looking through the filter of covetousness.

Tools to Protect

Our Heavenly Father has given us spiritual and natural tools to resist the enemy and his temptations. He gives us wisdom when we ask for it, strong marriage mentors, unlimited resources on protecting our marriage, and discernment to warn of danger. It is our responsibility to heed the warnings, use the tools, and fight a victorious battle for our marriages.

Along with the spiritual equipping, here are some very practical tools to help "Protect Your House."

· ·

TOOL #1
Beware of those who want to be "in the know" about your whole life.

· ·

There is no one in the church who should be your confidante or best friend outside of your husband. It makes for a bad mix when you confide in them about your struggle with issues, and then you are their spiritual leader on Sundays. As well, if you move to a new church or city, mark the person who wants to be the first to meet you or have you over for dinner. Mark those who say they are they ones who you can "share all your problems" with. (Put an asterisk by their name if they use the "I'm an intercessor and can pray for you" line!) Watch those who want to monopolize all your free time.

Most of the time, these types of people do not have pure motives.

· ·

TOOL #2

If your spouse warns you to stay away from someone, do it.

· ·

There are stop signs, yield signs, and maybe even caution signs. These signs usually come in the form of people—mainly your spouse—giving you a verbal warning. Heed the warning.

· ·

TOOL #3

Looks or age are not determining factors when determining a predator.

· ·

So many times, I have seen ministers or their wives fall prey to an affair; and once I saw the person who stole their allegiance, I have had to do a double-take and say, "Are you kidding me? What in the world did they see in this person?" The truth is, affairs happen on multiple levels, with sex usually being the "final" frontier. Maybe they were a better listener or had a way to feed their egos. Anybody can be used by Satan to destroy a marriage and a ministry, even if they put the "Ug" in U-G-L-Y! If they say the right words and push the right buttons, all of a sudden their looks—or age—become less important and irrelevant.

TOOL #4

Build hedges around your marriage and walk in integrity.

Some of these hedges may be built by things which seem small and insignificant, but those building blocks are still very important. Touch your spouse in public. Hold hands and hug. Have some physical contact when people are around. Be as Solomon's bride when she said:

> *"He brings me to the banquet hall, so everyone can see how much he loves me,"*

SONG OF SOLOMON 2:4 (TLB)

Randy and I established something years ago and have kept true to it. Neither one of us have business or casual meals with someone of the opposite sex without another party being present. In the same way, we do not counsel or visit with anyone of the opposite sex without another person being present. Our home and office computers have filters to keep Internet pornography out of our lives. We also question ourselves and each other about faithfulness. Each day, week, and month we have a personal agenda and schedule and know where each other is supposed to be at all times. Either one of us can be contacted by telephone if the need arises. These may sound like the workings of a control-freak husband or a very non-trusting wife; neither of which is true. All of these are hedges specifically designed to help protect our marriage, ministry, and personal integrity—and they work!

- -

TOOL #5
Guard yourself and don't abdicate your throne.

- -

Every time someone else does something you should be doing, you are giving up your rights which may not be very easy to regain. In our home, Randy should not be getting his "strokes" from anyone other than me. There should not be another woman doing his laundry, ironing his clothes (unless I hire them to do so), or taking my place next to his side. He should always know that what He needs is ME! There is no other woman who could ever love him as much or treat him as well as I do. I am his "Domestic Goddess," his queen, and I will not allow anyone else to sit on my throne—not even for a short time!

- -

TOOL #6
Guard your physical/sexual relationship.

- -

Sex is a gift from God and should not to be used to manipulate your spouse to get what you want. It should be a time of re-connecting your hearts and souls. If there is a sense that you and your husband are drawing apart, find the reasons and correct them. Are you too tired, too busy, or too distracted? Have you offended your spouse in some way? Are you honoring your personal relationship in public or have you made light of it? Have you gone too far and jested about sexual matters? Whatever the case may be, make the necessary adjustments and re-start your sexual intimacy.

Take the time to read the Song of Solomon again. Study it and get a true understanding for what Solomon was really saying to his Shulamite bride. While this book may be full of symbolism for the Bride of Christ and the church, it is also a wonderful sex manual inspired by God for his children. Use His manual to guard and continually build your relationship.

. . . .

TOOL #7

Give priority privileges.

. . . .

Let's face it. I have privileges and priorities concerning my husband that no one else can claim and vice-versa. For example, I have priority telephone and office privileges, as does Randy. What this means is either one of us can walk into each other's office at any time without being "buzzed through." No one on our staff is allowed to keep my telephone calls from him or his calls from me. Personal assistants are a huge blessing, but they know they will never stand between my husband and me.

No tool box is completely equipped with only seven tools, and no marriage is fully equipped with only seven hedges of protection built around it. Regardless of the tools you have at your disposal or the hedges you may build, just do something to make your marriage stronger. Do not put your marriage on "auto pilot" or make the mistake of thinking your marriage is infallible. Do not be deceived and think that Satan can't get to you or that your life is too perfect—it is not! It is always easier to look at the past and think, "What could I have done better?" My challenge to you is to look toward the future and plan to be better in your role as a wife, a lover, and a confidante.

SECTION III: *They Have Issues*

Footnote:

"If you want to forget your troubles, wear shoes that are
too tight."

11

How Do These Look?

MY ISSUE: *SAGE ADVICE FOR GIVING ADVICE*

$\mathcal{S}$ ometimes I wonder which I like better: buying a pair of shoes, or just trying them on! I love to look at them on my feet in the floor mirror, walk around the shoe department to see how they feel, and imagine which outfit would be the perfect match to. I stretch them, bend them, rock back on my heels, and stand on my tiptoes. Inevitably, I will also ask the opinion of anyone who happens to be near. Friend, family member, or total stranger, I don't care. I just want to know if they look good on me. However, if a stranger walks up out of nowhere and begins to volunteer information or compliments, it makes me wonder if they were sent on a mission by the salesperson. Why? Because compliments sell!

Compliments and suggestions are always nice; but when it comes down to it, I will do what I want to do. Advice, whether it is sought out by me or volunteered by others, is viewed the same in my mind. If I really want the shoes, I will buy them regardless of what they say, and no one can talk me out of it. Only a crisis like I don't have the cash, forgot my charge card, or I broke my ankle while trying on a pair with heels to high for me to walk in can change my mind. On that occasion, their advice might be followed, but only when there is no other choice.

Call me stubborn, strong-willed, headstrong, or whatever you would like. The truth is, whenever I get something in my mind, I soon decide that, that is the way it's going to be. I usually examine many possible scenarios and process what I would do in each case before making my final decision or judgment. Then, I have the responsibility to live out my decision—even if it is the wrong choice.

When I make a wrong purchase, it's easy to right the wrong simply by returning the shoes to the store where I bought them (with the receipt, of course). Unfortunately, wrong decisions in life are not quite as easy to correct. When I have made a wrong judgment call in life, I will either live with the decision or try to rectify it. This is when I become more receptive to the advice of others. The Bible explains it this way:

> *"A fool thinks he needs no advice, but a wise man listens to others."*

> **PROVERBS 12:15 (TLB)**

> *"Be humble, take advice, and become wise."*

> **PROVERBS 13:10 (TLB)**

"The advice of a wise man refreshes like water from a mountain spring. Those accepting it become aware of the pitfalls on ahead."

PROVERBS 13:14 (TLB)

The Problem-solving Pastor

People will often come to me and ask my advice concerning different things happening in their lives. This is not a problem for me. Some of these I can help; others, I cannot. Oftentimes, they come to me strictly because they think I have the "ear" of the pastor, and whatever I say or think will be exactly his advice as well. Let me tell you some shocking news: Randy and I do not always agree on everything, and my response might not necessarily be his. He is a thinker and a doer while I am a feeler. We don't always see eye-to-eye. You and your husband might be the same way. If so, that's okay. It's a good way to keep a checks-and-balances system.

Those who ask for a private session with me learn very quickly that I do not hold a degree in counseling. Legally, I can only give them sage advice, spiritual advice based on accounts from my own life experiences or my opinions. My opinions are just that—opinions. Obviously, I use God's Word first for guidance; however, there are things never directly addressed in the Bible. For instance, the Bible does not say smoking cigarettes is a sin, but it does tell us we should treat our bodies as the temple of the Lord. We are never told to not use cocaine, but are instructed to obey the laws of the land in which cocaine possession is illegal. God's Word never specifically mentions that R-rated movies are a sin; however, the Psalmist tells us that we should put no sinful thing before our eyes.[1]

People are looking for real answers, thus the need to know the Word of God! My secondary source has always been the core values of our particular church and/or any legalities involved. If I still cannot find the answer, then I will try to apply some good old common sense.

Randy has a very unique way of dealing with counseling issues which works great for him. We call it confrontational psychology. He confronts the issue, tells the person what to do to solve the issue, and sends them away with homework. He doesn't see them again until they have completed their assignments. Shockingly enough, it works and he rarely has to see the same people for the same issue more than once. That method works great for him but not for me. The key is to find the method which suits you and makes you feel comfortable.

A Unified Front

As I mentioned before, some seem to think my voice is a direct replica of the pastor. Because of this, I have to be very careful of my words (which is not always easy). Our thoughts, while not always exactly the same, should theoretically be in agreement, especially on vital family, social, and spiritual issues. Even if we do not agree in private, we will not disagree in public, as it can usurp the authority of his pastoral office and position.

Let me give you an example. We had to confront a spiritual issue in the home of one of our staff members. Through a series of events, I felt that his wife had been pushed to an emotional

---

1 Psalms 101:3

breaking point. Randy, however, thought that regardless of what had happened, she should continually represent her position of leadership and live above reproach (Remember, he is the "thinker;" I am the "feeler.") I felt all she needed was some time to regain her equilibrium and everything would be okay. He disagreed and thoroughly believed her issues were much more deep-seeded, and that she had totally turned her back on God. We obviously did not agree, but I never voiced my feelings to anyone other than him. There were two issues at stake here: one, the spiritual and emotional state of this lady and her family's wellbeing; and two, the agreement and integrity of the pastoral leadership. Honestly, I do not know to this day who was right or wrong. It never was an issue. Had I disagreed publicly, Randy's influence would have been tainted and undermined. Our public disunity would have created a monster, constantly raising its ugly head.

Step Into My Office

*E*ven though I have had some higher education in psychology and have lived through the "School of Hard Knocks," I am by no means an expert. I do not always have the right answer, or even the best answer; but prayerfully, I try to do my best with the information given to me. Still, I don't always succeed—and neither will you. When you do mess up, admit it, ask for forgiveness, and go on.

Again, Dr. Phil I am not, but there are some principles I have learned throughout the years when it comes to talking to people which I would love to pass on:

1. **Often, people don't even want advice.** More times than

not, advice is not what people are seeking, even though it is what they are asking for. What they really want is someone to vent their frustrations to in a safe place or for someone to agree with their actions or feelings. It's okay, as long as you know this up front and can be prepared.

2. **Take good notes.** When people come to see you, keep good notes, so you can read back through what they have said and get a clearer understanding of their issues. This does two things. First, it communicates to them that you are truly interested in their issues. Secondly, it will be especially helpful if you are to see them again. It is important to make sure you keep those notes under lock and key. They are private and confidential. Anyone else reading them, whether by accident or on purpose, could break the person's trust and confidence in you. More importantly, it could damage your integrity to counsel people in the future, and that is never a good thing.

3. **Just listen until the tirade is over.** Most professional counselors will tell you that the majority of their job is to be a good listener. I agree. Sometimes, the best things you can say is, "M-m-mmm. Ah-hhh. Oh-h-h-hhh. Uh-huh. Really?" When they have finished their tirade, they think you have really helped them, when in all actuality, all you really did was listen.

4. **Try reflective listening.** This is a technique which involves not only listening, but repeating back everything exactly as they have said it. Next, rephrase their words. Ask them if what you have said is what they really meant. Many times people

have feelings in their heart; but by the time they attempt to express them in words, they become confused and guarded. Repeating what you have heard and asking questions helps to bring clarity not only to you, but also to them. Remember, many problems are the result of miscommunication. For instance, in the event of a marriage counseling session, if something they were really feeling was miscommunicated to their spouse, that could be the beginning of their problem—or at least, part of it!

5. **Be prepared for difficult and traumatic issues.** Try to listen without becoming emotionally involved—especially if the problem involves another person in your church. You do not want to exhibit a biased opinion or make a judgment call before you have all the facts. Information is power!

6. **Turn over legal problems to those who are qualified.** If the issue you are presented involves any perceived legalities, take it to someone who is licensed to handle them. For instance, in the state of Georgia, ministers are mandated reporting agents. This means we are required by law to report even suspected molestation or abuse of a child to the authorities. It does not matter how long ago it happened or when the abuser accepted Christ; we are still mandated to report it. The authorities, then, have to make the decision to investigate and/or press charges. Personally, I have no problem reporting any abuser even if his/her sin is under the Blood of Jesus. The perpetrator needs to be handed over to the hands of our justice system and pay the price—if any— for their wrongdoing. They can remain a Christian in prison

and have a ministry of God's forgiveness.

7. **Offer a safe place for domestic abuse.** If you haven't been in the ministry very long, it will not take much time for you to figure out that Christian families also deal with some of the same domestic issues of those in the world. When faced with domestic abuse, be bold to tell the person who is being abused to find a safe place. Even if it means leaving the spouse for a time; they just need to get safe. This is not necessarily counsel to file for a divorce, but rather a place of safety for a season.

8. **Never be afraid to say, "I don't know."** If you ever have to say this (and I do often), follow it up with the assurance you will try to find an answer. No one has all the answers all the time; and if they claim to, maybe they need to seek counseling for lying! People will respect your honesty and openness.

9. **Watch for the time leeches.** Whether you are at the altar, in public, or on the telephone, someone will always be there to try and suck the life right out of you by demanding a large portion of your attention. There are ways, however, to stop this manipulation:

   * Offer to meet them in a private setting during the week.

   * Excuse yourself from the conversation and tell them to call you on Monday to finish.

* Give someone a "heads up" that you might need to be rescued from a lengthy conversation.

* Find another appointment to go to.

10. **Listen with your heart and your spirit.** People will go through certain situations which seem very unfair. There will be times where someone may appear to be an innocent party, and we may unwittingly "side" with them. There is a major distinction between offering sympathy to someone who is hurting and empathizing with their situation. The difference is sympathy offers compassion, while empathy leads you to vicariously feel what the person is feeling—putting yourself in their situation and becoming too emotionally involved. You begin to feel their emotions and take on their offense. At this point, you may lose your perspective and the ability to remain unbiased.

    On the other hand, when you listen with your heart and spirit, it allows you to give Godly counsel based on the Word of God, regardless of your feelings. It does not matter how you feel about what someone else may be experiencing. God can see past the emotions and the possible innocence of the moment. He sees past the unfairness of it all and determines what His child can learn from the experience. As a spiritual counselor, always remember that God is sovereign, and you must trust Him to do what is best.

11. **Learn the "golden rule" of counseling.** It is this: no one cares how much you know, until they know how much you care. The best way to help people is to love them and to build relationships first. The results are amazing.

- -

No one cares how much you know, until they know how much you care.

- -

12. **Guard your words.** Words that soak into people's ears are whispered, not yelled. Remember, you cannot unsay a cruel thing. Chose your words carefully and make sure your counsel is Word-inspired, not opinion inspired.

13. **Don't be afraid to confront.** If you feel the person you are listening to is wrong, do not be afraid to tell them. Of course, exercise Ephesians 4:15 and always "speak the truth in love." We live in a society with generally no backbone that is conditioned to be more "politically correct" than honest. God's Word is not a politically correct document. Sin is still spelled S-I-N. In the Bible, people were called what they were: prostitutes, whoremongers, adulterers, sorcerers, hypocrites, depraved—just to name a few. When you do have to confront a sin issue, look for signs of repentance and remorse in the person and speak words of mercy, forgiveness, and restoration.

Footnote:

"The shoe that fits one person pinches another."

12

Too Many Shoes, Not Enough Feet

MY ISSUE: *OVERCOMMITMENT IN MINISTRY*

ometimes after Christmas, we go on a short family trip just for fun. One year, after returning from one such trip, we arrived at the airport to find our luggage had not made the trip with us. We searched for more than three hours and found two of the four missing pieces. The next day, one more piece was delivered. To this day, the other piece has never been found nor returned to us. I was commiserating with a friend of mine shortly after we realized the luggage was irretrievably lost and stated that the most important thing missing was my new pair of shoes. "Bless your little heart," she laughed, "It's not like you don't have any others to wear!" I then realized how ridiculous it all sounded. You see, she has seen my closet and knows first-hand how many pairs of shoes I own. Actually, she knows I really have too many.

After that conversation, I discarded nine pairs of shoes. But just about the time I got rid of them, I was making room for the pair I was to buy the following week. (If you haven't noticed, I love shoes!)

Think about it. Aren't we the same with the issues in our lives? Just about the time we get rid of some lingering issues we add more; and find out once again, we have way too many *issues*!

If I Had Only Known

Have you ever asked yourself, "What does God expect from me in the ministry? Does He require more from me than from anyone else? How can I determine exactly where to draw the line and say, 'Enough already?'" For me, just entering into the ministry, I would have given all the money in world to someone if they could have answered these (and a 1000 more) questions. Honestly, I didn't even know I had the freedom to ask. If someone would have helped me, I know it would have saved me from a lot of heartache and much misspent energy.

Well, like I said before, I have learned a lot through life experiences, trial-and-error, the "School of Hard Knocks," and much prayer. There was no one to guide me. So, I want to share a few valuable lessons—and regrets—I have encountered in my journey through the world of ministry.

1. **I just about worked myself to death in our first church.**
   Like every other new bride entering into the ministry, I thought in order to "earn" my title as a "good pastor's wife,"

I was to do everything—and I mean EVERYTHING—I was asked to do. The word "no" was not to be found in my vocabulary! I truly thought this was what God required of me and every other minister's wife. It was not until a few years later when I finally came to the realization that this idea of working ourselves to death originated from the pit of hell. Just because I was busy doing the work of the Lord, He did not make me any more spiritual than those who are not as busy. It only meant they are working smarter, not harder, than I was. Not only was I working myself crazy, I was also making it practically impossible for the next pastor's wife to follow in my footsteps. My mantra was not, "May all who come behind me find me faithful," but instead it was, "May all who come behind me find me half-dead!" At times, I thought I was living up to this self-imposed tune far too well.

2. **I wished my husband had known he was not married to Superwoman.** Randy truly thought I could do all things—and do them all well. If he saw a job that needed to be done, he gave it to me; knowing I would not rest until it was completed to his liking. At this time, I did not possess the gift of delegation, so everything was done by me. It was not Randy's fault. It was mine. My desire to be a good wife was rooted in works that were measurable, things that could be seen. If I had only allowed Randy to protect me from myself . . . but again, I just didn't know.

3. **I regret not helping our first church to understand the role of the pastor's wife.** They were great people, and I believe they would have understood and helped me to be the

best I could be. The problem did not lie with them, but rather with me. Part of my goal was to seem invincible. (Again, this was due to the fact that it was all I knew at the time.) I had watched my own mother for years seem to have no cracks in her armor, and I was determined to be just like her: "all things to all people." The church's expectations of me were based on my youthful vigor, not in reality.

Room in the Closet

To be in the ministry means God has determined something out of the ordinary for your life. You are called to complete a special assignment that you alone can assess and know how to accomplish. This anointing is in you, whether you are a minister's wife or a lay person. God will send people across your path who will be touched because of who and what you are. Among numerous things, you will be a burden-bearer for your husband—your equal partner in the ministry God has called you *both* to. The anointing of God's call will be one of the most precious things you will ever experience. Never take for granted the mantle placed upon your life.

When you try to do ministry within your own strength, you turn His mantle into your yoke.

Don't replace the space in the closet with new shoes—new issues. When you try to do ministry within your own strength, you turn *His* mantle into *your* yoke. This is not God's plan. His yoke is easy, and His burden is light.

Look around your church environment right now. What do you see that needs to be done? Is it a burden on your heart? Do you find yourself trying to think of solutions and different ways to solve the problem? This is God's gifting within you.

The most important thing you can do is to learn to recognize and obey God's voice.

Not only has God called you to a broad ministry and influence, but there will be specific things which God will lay upon your heart. The most important thing you can do is to learn to recognize and obey God's voice. Many times, there will be those who will say, "God wants you to do this," or "God's will is for this to happen." When it concerns your life, only you can determine what God is saying or where God is leading.

Learning to recognize God's voice comes primarily by spending quality, personal time with Him. As with any relationship, the more time you spend with God, the better you will get to know Him, His heart, and His voice. You will also recognize imposters of God's voice, thus making it easier to clearly define when He is speaking, and where He is leading.

Often, someone will come to me with an idea of a new ministry which *they* think I need to begin. I usually "test the waters" during our conversation to see if it is a confirmation to my spirit or something from outer space (hypothetically speaking, of course). If it is a confirmation, I will act on it. More often than not, God had laid this ministry and area of need upon their hearts, and they are trying to convince me to do it. They rationalize it by thinking that if I will take the responsibility, it will release them from the necessity of doing it. WRONG! I am very cautious about taking an idea from someone and moving forward with it myself. If I allow myself to do everything suggested to me, I would just be creating things for me to do and not making disciples. I usually place the burden back on their shoulders with a few well-spoken words like this, "What a great idea! I see you have really been thinking and praying about this. Right now, I have just about as much as I can handle, but I believe God has really placed this idea in you to accomplish. How can I help you get started?" I have learned that when God calls someone to do a job, no amount of talking about it will release the burden; and no matter how many others are doing it, they still have the God-given desire to do it.

When God calls someone to do a job, no amount of talking about it will release their God-given burden to do it.

My Assignment

When we first moved to Griffin, Georgia, I saw a problem which needed to be fixed. It was in our young married couples' ministry. There was no fellowship for them whatsoever. No one was helping them to stay married, teaching them the disciplines of child-rearing, helping them with finances—among other vital issues young married couples face. As a result, we began to see a lot of dysfunction in the church. Many of our couples began to experience major marriage and family problems, near bankruptcies, out of control children, and feelings of isolation.

I started praying for solutions and seeking ways to help. I began to look for someone with a successful marriage to mentor these couples. Out of the blue one day, my husband looked at me and said, "Jelly, God has placed this burden on *your* heart. Stop trying to find someone to fix the problem. You are part of the solution. Start a Sunday School class and begin helping these couples." This really frightened me, because I had never taught adults, just children. However, Randy's statement resonated in my spirit and confirmed what the Lord was already trying to tell me. So, for the next 11 years, I taught the young married couples in our church the principles of marriage and family. Because their families were better equipped for conflict and were equipped with viable solutions, the core of our families became stronger; and they, in turn, began to mentor other young couples.

In my twelfth year of teaching this class, someone came to me with a burden to teach young couples how to build stronger families. I had already felt God was releasing me, and I welcomed the opportunity to hand over the Sunday School class to someone else. My ego was not crushed, nor did I feel as though I was being replaced. It was the ministry coming full-circle in that I was now making disciples of others and helping them to fulfill their call and desire to work for the Lord.

If there is one thing I would want to get across, it is this: always remember, this is not just *your* ministry. It is a ministry team, and it is the work of the Lord. Don't think just because you started something, it belongs solely to you. The Kingdom of God is not about ownership; it's about servitude and ministry to others. God has entrusted people to you to teach, train, and then release into the things He has poured into their hearts through your work. This is one of the ways God uses multiplication!

. . . .

Always remember, this is not just your

ministry.

. . . .

"God, Are You Sure?"

After I stopped teaching the couples' Sunday School class, I began to think of all the other things which needed my attention (or so I thought!), and whether or not I wanted to do them. The list was endless. I could work in the nursery, go back to teaching children, begin to co-teach with my husband, start another class, etcetera.

You see, there will always be a job—whether it is your first choice or not—which needs to be done. The answer I was looking for came from God loud and clear: DO NOTHING! My job was to sit and be a resource, if needed, to those who had been trained and called for specific ministries. Seeing as I have been a busy person in the ministry all of my life, I didn't quite know how I was going to handle this new assignment. But, I knew it was God's voice. Honestly, I am relishing in the place God has me in right now. It is wonderful to have the opportunity to sit and listen without the pressure of preparation. If I had held on to my class, it would have deprived someone of the ministry opportunity which God had called them to do. If I had started another class, it would not have been the right time or the right format. God called me to wait; and much to my surprise, I like this kind of waiting.

Let me end this chapter by giving some balance. Wherever God has placed you in ministry, there is a job for you to do. You are not called to sit around and watch everyone else do it; you are called to work. Had Adam protected his wife (that's for another book!) and Eve not sinned, there would be no such thing as WORK. How do you spell ministry? W.O.R.K.! Absolutely right. Only in eternity will our need for work cease. The Bible encourages us, *"Whatever your hand finds to do, do it with all your might . . ."*[1] Be pleasing to the Father in your work, but don't kill yourself or waste your life in the process. Over-commitment will do this to you.

It is necessary to clean out the old shoes, but not entirely necessary to fill up the closet again!

---

1 See Ecclesiastes 9:10

Footnote:

"One of these days these boots are gonna

walk all over you."

Les Hazelwood

From the song, "These Boots are Made for Walking"

13

Rubber Soles

MY ISSUE: *BOUNCING BACK*

*I*n the late 1990's, Walt Disney Productions® produced a movie entitled, *Flubber.* I don't remember much about the movie except that Flubber was a product which enabled extraordinary "bounce" and increased the resiliency of a particular item. In one scene, someone put Flubber on their shoes during a basketball game and immediately became the star player, as their ability to jump and rebound soared above everyone else's. It wasn't just a few moments later that everyone wanted Flubber so they, too could "bounce."

Many times, I would really like to have some of that resiliency. If only I could find some of those Flubber shoes! Then, I would become the star pastor's wife, doing everything I was "supposed" to do and never get tired. I can see it now. There I am bouncing around the church at lightning speed, decorating faster than a speeding bullet, producing the church bulletin faster than my computer, rebounding my way out of the circumstances that could cause me pain and disappointment; miraculously bouncing back from pain to a place of mental, spiritual, and emotional health. The possibilities would be endless! Unfortunately, this is not reality.

. . . .

Life is about how well you can bounce.

. . . .

Flubber is a myth. There is no product designed to provide "bounce" and resiliency in life. Those, my friend, are only achieved through hard work. Life is not about how high you can climb or how fast you can run, but it is about how well you can bounce.

There is something better than Flubber to help you bounce in real life—the Holy Spirit. Even if you could have the magical Flubber shoes, they would have to be coated with the oil of the Holy Spirit. That oil seeps through your shoes into your feet and ankles, all the way up your legs, and into your heart. Before you know it, it has made its way into your bloodstream and permeated every part of your body and spirit. Only when you allow this to happen is when you can really be truly resilient.

Ministry is a place where we have the immense opportunity to be wounded. We must frequently put our own lives on the line for others, and we must live a life of continuous sacrifice. No matter how much we watch our words, actions, and attitudes, we can inevitably say, do, and think the wrong things at the wrong times. By making ourselves available to those we serve, we also make ourselves vulnerable. Our vulnerability increases our potential to be hurt. It also increases our potential for every imaginable victory to be won in hard-fought war.

What's Wrong with the Nursery?

$\mathscr{I}$ distinctly remember one Sunday morning when God visited our service in a new and fresh way. People who were carrying hurts and heartaches began to let go of their pasts in a way completely orchestrated by the Holy Spirit. Others came to the altar for salvation. Lives were changed that day and, as pastors, we were on cloud nine to see the power of God moving so mightily in our little church. As we were leaving the service, I saw one of our ladies and wanted to rejoice with her about all we had just experienced. She seemed a little aggravated because she had just spent the whole service doing nursery duty. "Oh, I'm so sorry," I said. "It seems that every time we have a good service, you are on nursery duty." *Wrong thing to say.*

- -

Ministry is a place where we have the immense opportunity to be wounded.

- -

A few days later, my husband was met at our front door by this same woman who walked right past him and entered our home screaming like a wild banshee. "Just what did you mean by your statement?" she questioned. "Do you think I have something in my spirit that hinders the services? Do you believe the only time God can move is when I am in the nursery? If this is what you really think, then my family and I will just find another church."

No amount of reasoning could change her mind because she

had already chosen to be offended. I was so deeply wounded by her words and actions that I wept and prayed for many hours trying to understand where I had gone wrong. I kept asking myself, "What could I have said differently that would not have offended her?" My words had not been motivated by anything other than conversation about the goodness of our Father.

What I didn't know at the time was the fact that she did not like babies or children, and she hated working in the nursery! So, before I ever said one word to her, she was already mad because she had missed such a good church service. Slightly ironic, isn't it? If anybody needed that service, she did. In the end, she stayed in the church and became a solid member with much devotion to prayer. She never became a close confidante, but I did learn to appreciate her and her idiosyncrasies. Needless to say, we took her off the nursery duty roster!

The Age-Old Question

When this lady came and busted down our door, I was faced with a decision. Her reactions were a result of my ill-timed words. My words caused her pain, and her words caused me pain. Now I had a choice to make. Was I going to forgive her or choose to hold the pain close to my heart? Forgiveness is a decision, a choice; but healing takes time. I did choose to forgive, but it was many days before I could think about this whole scenario without feeling the same pain.

My sister, Linda, is also a pastor's wife. A few years ago, they were in a pastorate of a highly dysfunctional church. Through a series of events, the church board decided my sister and her family were no longer needed as pastors and "dis-elected" them. This decision left them with no job, no home, no money, and Linda was ready to deliver a new baby. For many months after their last service, Linda was extremely angry at the church board. Every time she thought about them, her blood pressure would rise. She would become angry all over again, and her anger would become almost tangible and palpable—affecting everyone around her.

Forgiveness is a decision, a choice; but healing takes time.

I remember one occasion when Linda went into a verbal tirade concerning how the church and the board of elders were mistreating her and her family. During our conversation, my husband stopped her and reminded her that we were not a part of the board; we were her friends, not her enemies. She then realized her anger was being directed toward anyone who listened. When she began to pray about her pain and anger, the Holy Spirit quickly assured her that He was keeping an account of the wrongs which had been committed against them. Linda, then, made a choice to begin the process of forgiveness. In doing so, she let go of her right to be angry and to be the instrument of God's vengeance. She even tore up her hit list! (I really don't think she ever had one, though.)

Years later, she was walking through a local department store and saw someone who had been on that church board. She immediately stopped and looked deep into her emotions for some harsh words to say, but she could not find them! This was her defining moment, when she knew she had truly forgiven them. Linda had made a choice to forgive; and through her decision, healing had come to her own spirit. The decision to forgive—even when circumstances seem unforgivable—is a huge step in being able to bounce back from hurt. Those who choose not to forgive become bitter and lifeless. For us who choose forgiveness, we might get old, but don't have to be full of bitterness and resentment.

"Wounded" or "Scarred"?

Someone once said that ministers and their wives are the "walking wounded." I choose to be the "walking scarred" instead. Which is better: to live your life with an oozing, painful wound or to just carry the scars from those wounds? Scars signify there have been wounds, sometimes massive wounds, but they also remind us how they have been healed and no longer possess the power to hurt. Actually, scar tissue is stronger than the original area before it was wounded.

As a minister's wife, yes, it is inevitable that you have been hurt. Yes, you have been wronged. And, no, you did not deserve what happened. Life is full of pain to those who serve in the ministry *and* to those who do not, but never forget that life is also full of joy. My advice: look at the joy, not the heartache.

So, what can you do when ministry hurts? Again, this is not an extensive list, but some areas to consider which will help ease the pain.

1. **Pain reminds you to keep your eyes on Jesus.** Always remain focused on the eternal.

2. **Remember that brokenness and tears do not go unnoticed in God's Kingdom.** When you embrace suffering, you gain maturity. Maturity leads to perseverance and perseverance to character. The character you gain from going through hurt and disappointment will lead you into hope for the future. You will have a perspective that only comes from a close relationship with Jesus Christ. Romans 5:1-5 says:

    > *"Therefore, having been justified by faith, we have peace with God through our Lord Jesus Christ, through whom also we have access by faith into this grace in which we stand, and rejoice in hope of the glory of God. And not only that, but we also glory in tribulations, knowing that tribulation produces perseverance; and perseverance, character; and character, hope. Now hope does not disappoint, because the love of God has been poured out in our hearts by the Holy Spirit who was given to us."*

3. **Realize there are questions which cannot be answered.** You may never be able to answer the questions of "why?" or "why me?" Just let them go.

4. **Don't carry grudges.** It never takes a big person to carry a grudge. When you forgive someone and let go of the grudge, it messes with the other party's head. This is the best revenge—if you feel you need it.

5. **Don't allow people and their wrongs to rent space in your mind.** You already have enough in storage up there and have

no time for a yard sale! Post a "No Vacancy" sign on you for those who are offended or those who offend you!

6. **Everything is temporary.** ". . . and it came to pass . . ." The Word never tells us ". . . and it came to stay." This is all temporary. It will not last forever.

7. **Sometimes broken relationships cannot be repaired.** In Genesis 13:5-12, Abram and Lot had a problem. Rather than sever the relationship, God allowed them to "put some space between them." Lot went to Jordan, and Abram went to Canaan. Later, Abram rescued Lot from captivity. When help was needed, even though there had been a difference of opinion, Abram was there to help.

* * *

You cannot change people or their actions, but you can control your response to them.

* * *

In this world, there are many different personalities and different values. You cannot change people or their actions, but you can control your response to them. Sometimes you might just need space and time. You need to move away— not necessarily to another town, but remove yourself from the situation for a time. Take a break, refocus, and get a better perspective. No matter what, always be available when needed. Had Abram harbored his anger towards Lot, he would not have been properly able to minister to Lot's needs when he was in trouble.

8. **Read Psalm 55.** Make a copy of the whole chapter and tape it to your mirror. Pull out key verses, write them on an index card and tape it to the dashboard of your car, the nightstand by your bed, the desk in your office—wherever you spend time and can quickly read a verse of Scripture. If you really need to, tape them to your forehead or sleep with them in your pillowcase. Do whatever you need to do! Always remind yourself that God is your defense, and He is where you will put your trust.

Bouncing back is not all that easy, nor is it impossible. The first step is your *desire* to rebound from the hurt and pain. To begin the process, find a place alone with God and allow Him to give you the desire to get through the hurt. Once you've made the decision in your heart, the Holy Spirit will come and start the healing, rebounding process. Allow Him to do His work. It's much better than Flubber!

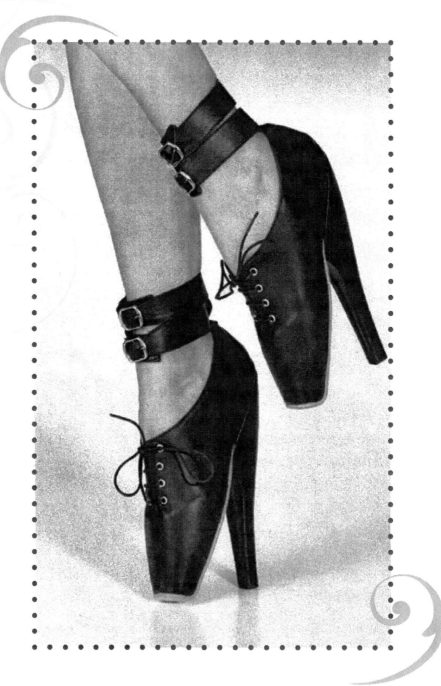

Footnote:

"Painful shoes (issues) can change the way we walk."

14

Painful Shoes

My Issue: Grieving with Those We Love

*W*hen I was younger, I had a problem with shoes: the cuter they were, the more I wanted them! Whether they actually ever fit was never a consideration. No heel was too tall or too spiked, no toe was too narrow or too short, no instep was too unsupported or too high. The only important issue to me was that the shoes were really cute—any color, any style, any size. I would buy these shoes and wear them regardless of the pain. I went to work in my cute, but painful, shoes hoping that by wearing them all day, I would somehow "break them in." But, they were breaking me! Then, I figured they would not only be cute, but also painless. Never happened.

I could never fully understand why the comfort of shoes was unimportant to me, until I began to examine my thought process and found the answer. It was my parents' fault. Yes, that's right! I was not to blame. (Don't you just love being able to blame your issues on someone else?) They programmed me to wear painful shoes. How? Well, "Money," as my Dad would say, "does not grow on trees. We can make these shoes work just a little bit longer." So, even as a child, I had to wear shoes that were not the most comfortable. I never actually cut out any of the toes, so I could wear them longer. But, I do remember buying sandals at Easter, so I could wear them all summer or until the weather was too cold. And, if by chance my sandal straps broke, they went to the repair shop, not the garbage can.

Not only was it common for me to wear shoes that were too small, it wasn't unusual for me to wear ones that were too big. My parents had to accommodate for my growth, so they usually bought my shoes larger than my foot. Or, I acquired the hand-me-downs from my sister. I learned all the shoe tricks at a young age: putting tissue in the toes so they wouldn't slip, using Band-Aids® on the backs of my shoes or heel to help prevent blisters, etcetera. In our house, with three growing girls, we went through a steady supply of Kleenex® and Band-Aids®. You can imagine my excitement when my parents finally decided that my foot would never be as long as my sister's. I could finally say "goodbye" to tissues and bandages and "hello" to my own pairs of shoes. That was a good day!

Oh, the pain we have suffered to have cute shoes: bunions, calluses, crooked toes, ingrown toenails, and that funky-looking misshapen bone next to our big toes! Now that I'm older (and, hopefully, wiser!), I no longer expect to grow into shoes or break them in. If they don't feel good when I put them on, they do not go into my shopping bag. I only wear shoes that feel good. Period. As I grow older, I avoid any pain in my feet. Even my bedroom slippers must feel good, or they, too will find a new home. I give away or throw away any pair of shoes which inflict pain!

It's amazing how we try to avoid pain, isn't it? How nice life would be if we could just give away, throw away, or return all the things which cause us pain. Just as our feet have been molded by painful shoes, our lives are often molded by painful issues. Sometimes, our feet must go through surgical procedures or therapy. We may even have to wear special shoes and hosiery, spend an extended amount of time elevating our feet, or completely stay off of them for a while—all due to the pain.

Our lives are very similar. There are times when we have to allow God to perform a surgical procedure or therapy on our heart to help remove the pain caused by our "issues." There may be a time of extended rest required or complete removal from a painful situation. Any of these antidotes can be the beginning of a true healing process.

Facing the Inevitable

No matter how hard we try, we can never avoid pain and grief. It's the part of life we do not like to think about, as it contradicts the whole "rose garden" theology. Too many times we believe that if we do everything right—treat everyone kindly, sacrifice our time, read and practice the Word of God, and keep ourselves from sin—then, we will never have difficulty in life. In many faith circles, to even say the word "heartache" is considered a "bad confession."

Well, whether we confess it or not, pain and heartache in life is inevitable. There will be grief. Some things will have no logical answer in which we can just explain away or confess our way out of. King Solomon told us in Ecclesiastes chapter three that there is a time for everything. There is a time for laughter and a time for mourning.

We all love the laughter but want to pretend that the mourning does not, or cannot, affect us.

I truly believe no one can ever really be prepared for grief. There are no classes in seminary which offer step-by-step instructions of what to do when tragedy strikes. Often, it will happen when we are least prepared or least expectant. When a tragedy comes, it is not the time to go "Bible dipping" for the right things to say. I once heard an elder minister say, *"If you put the Word of God in you when you don't seem to need it, it will be there when*

When a tragedy comes, it is not the time to go "Bible dipping" for the right things to say.

---

you do need it!" Immersing yourself daily in the presence, the power, and the Word of God is the only way to truly prepare for difficult times. A daily dose of God's Word will not only equip you for tough times, but it will also serve as a reminder how He will carry you through by the words already planted in your heart. When you chart your course before the storm, there is a great amount of trust in God's plan when storms arise.

> *"Praise be to the God and Father of our Lord Jesus Christ,*
> *the Father of all compassion and the God of all comfort,*
> *who comforts us in all our troubles, so that we can comfort*
> *those in any trouble with the comfort that we ourselves have*

received from God . . . If we are distressed, it is for your comfort and salvation; if we are comforted, it is for your comfort, which produces in you patient endurance of the same sufferings we suffer. And our hope for you is firm, because we know that just as you share in our sufferings, so also you share in our comfort."

2 CORINTHIANS 1:3-4, 6-7 (NIV)

Grieving and pain can come in many forms; like a broken relationship with a friend, a parent, a spouse, or one of your children. It may occur through a job change, the closing of a business, a new position, or even a necessary relocation. A woman who is barren and unable to birth children could experience much grief and heartache, feeling as though she is inadequate for her husband. Grieving can also come to us because of the death of a loved one—expected or unexpected. Even church-related issues can bring much disappointment and heartache. Regardless of why one encounters grief, as a ministry family, you must understand that you will encounter it with them. It may be someone in your church or in a personal/family relationship outside your immediate church family. Your effectiveness of ministering to the person in grief is directly related to how well you deal with and recover from the impending situation yourself. Preparation is imperative!

Too Many Questions—Not Enough Answers

The age-old question asked when anyone faces tragedy is one word: "Why?" I believe the first thing ministers need to do is to steer people away from the "blame game." When an unexpected circumstance happens, it is always easier to blame someone or something else. People usually take one of four roads in the "blame game":

1. **They blame God.** When people blame God, they begin to lock Him out of their lives, negating the possibility for healing to come. Questions like: "Why did God let this happen to me? Why didn't God stop this from happening? Why is God punishing me?" are all commonly heard or felt.

2. **They blame Satan.** Sometimes people who experience grief and loss hold the devil responsible for their pain and heartache, not man. At times, this can over emphasize the responsibility which sin may have played.

3. **They blame mankind.** This is also referred to as our "sinful world" or "fallen nature." In most occasions, this blame usually results in people taking matters into their own hands to do something about it.

4. **They blame themselves.** Most people who blame themselves start looking for something lacking in their own life which caused the tragedy. "This wouldn't have happened if I would have just prayed more." "Do I have a lack of faith?" "Was I in sin, and this is God's punishment on me?" Again, more questions than answers.

Coupled with the question of "Why?" is usually the question, "What will I do now?" Every situation and circumstance is unique—

and again, there are no patented answers. A few years ago, there was a popular movie about a widower whose son wanted a new mother. While talking with a radio talk show personality, she asked the boy, "What are you going to do now?" He responded by saying, "I will get up every morning. I will breathe in and out. And, someday, I won't have to remind myself to get up every morning and to breathe in and out."

Many times, I, too have found myself repeating these words in attempt to answer the question, "What next?" Time truly does provide a measure of healing, if people are willing to embrace the opportunity to heal and go on with the abundant life God has promised.

Life After Tragedy

Many years ago, we had a wonderful staff member whose wife left him after a very stressful time in their home, their marriage, and also in the church. She left behind two beautiful young girls and moved in with another woman. Needless to say, both he and the girls were devastated. He was an innocent party who loved his wife and never envisioned losing his marriage and becoming a single, custodial parent. As a ministry team, we were faced with some decisions. We decided to embrace this minister, believe in him and the call of God on his life, and allow him to continue his ministry functions. It was the right decision. Today, he is happily remarried, and both of his daughters have earned their college degrees. He has been named Teacher of the Year in his home state and has been a finalist as the National Teacher of the Year. He has received his doctorate degree and is the dean of education at a Christian university, plus he leads a very successful ministry for single parents at his local church.

This man looked at us in the midst of major turmoil and thought, "What now? Where do I go? What do I do?" Everything about his life—both personal and ministerial—seemed to be crashing in all around him. He could have been destroyed during his time of grief and pain. Instead, he chose to walk the road of heartache and not stay in one place either emotionally or spiritually. This was the road to victory! It was not a quick road to recovery, nor was it easy; but God was faithful to bring new life and complete restoration.

The road to recovery is not quick, but God is faithful to bring complete restoration.

Our church is filled with people who work in the airline industry. After the terrorist attack on September 11, 2001, many of these people, and the businesses they worked for, suffered catastrophic financial loss. I remember hearing, "What do I do know?" over and over and over again. Although some were prepared for an economic crunch, many were financially destroyed. These families had not overextended themselves and lived within their financial means; but now, without warning, they found themselves struggling to simply pay their necessary bills. Even though Randy and I did not have the answers to the reoccurring question, we did encourage these people to remain faithful to God even during this tough time.

In the end, many of these precious people were able to recoup much of their original loss. Others were forced to follow their secret dream! During this time of loss, God brought their secret dreams into the light and provided the steps to see those dreams finally become a reality. And why not? The thing which they had previously been afraid to try no longer held any fear, because they knew they had nothing to lose. Some were glad they were "pushed out of the nest" and made to fly on their own!

Personal Experiences

Through the years, Randy and I have had to deal with our fair share of unexpected tragedy and misfortunes. When we began in the ministry together, no one ever prepared us for the things we would eventually face and be called upon to help minister and guide people through. It has been a tough, learning experience; but in the end, God has taught us how to adapt and be effective in every situation. Each case has been very unique, requiring specific paths of healing and restoration. Here are a few examples:

* One of our former staff members nursed her mother through years of Alzheimer's disease. This beautiful, Godly, and gracious southern lady spent the last years of her life bedridden and cursing at those who attended to her. Before she died, memories of this lady as a beautiful, nurturing mother were erased by this fatal disease. Her precious daughter grieved the loss of her mother for years before death ever claimed her life.

* A close friend of mine came home from work one day to find

that her 14 year-old daughter had committed suicide. There were no threats, no signs, no notes; just one gunshot, and her life was over. For years, my friend made her daughter's room a shrine of her short life, like she was expecting her to walk through the door at any minute. She even spoke of her daughter in the present tense, not in the past. After years of prayer and counseling, this family made enough progress to move out of the home where their daughter had tragically ended her life and began the process of moving on with their lives.

* Our daughter's best friend, Bethany, committed to spend the summer before her sophomore year on the mission field in Mexico. She was a Godly young lady, a very talented musician and vocalist, plus a whole bundle of mischievous fun. One night after a very successful crusade in Monterrey, her team was headed home when the van she was riding in blew a tire. Their van rolled several times, instantly killing four of the team members. Bethany received massive injuries and, after lingering for two days on life support system, never regained consciousness. The grief her family felt—along with our own family and church family—was, at times, unbearable. Her family's grief was met with some joy as they selected to donate all of her organs to those who were in need. It was exactly what Bethany would have wanted, as her life was dedicated to helping others.

* As we prepared for Bethany's memorial service, I received a frantic call from a local pastor whom my husband was mentoring. Six people from his church were returning from a youth trip when a transfer truck collided with their van,

exploding and killing five people.

* Our youngest daughter was premature, and her doctors said she would never live a normal life. When God healed her, he gave her a new set of lungs and a brilliant mind.

* When our oldest daughter was 19, she became bitter toward the things of God and left home one day while we were away. We did not see her for six months, but we knew God had a destiny for her life which would draw her back to God and to her family. Randy and I had tried our best to be good, Godly parents and build a strong family in the ministry; but at that moment, it all seemed a complete failure. We learned through our grieving what it really meant to trust God and His Word. One thing we held on to was the fact that God loved her more than we did, and He held her future. First Corinthians 13:12 became more real to me during this time when I began to meditate on the fact that "we now see through a glass darkly but then someday, face to face" (KJV). Eventually, she came back to Christ, returned home, and finished her training to be in full-time ministry. Today, she is a licensed minister!

* In October 2005, our daughter received a call from her fiancé's employer saying that he had become ill at work. They thought it would be a good idea for her to come and pick him up, so he could recover at home. Through the impression of the Holy Spirit, my husband told her to bring Bruce to our home so we could attend to anything he might need while he was recovering. I cannot tell you the depths of our grief when we discovered that Bruce had died during the night

from a massive heart attack in our home.

I would like to say I have all the answers for all the bad things which have happened in our life. I would also like to be able to point out certain factors to which we can attribute the blame. But, the truth is, I do not have many answers at all. One thing I do know is when you are in the ministry, people will expect you to say the right thing at the right time and will look to you for answers which you may not have. People view their spiritual leaders as those who have a direct line to God and know His character. What makes this more difficult is when you have to hold up the hands of those around you while you are dealing with your own feelings of grief, shock, devastation, anger, or emotional and spiritual emptiness. It is at these times where God's grace is sufficient and made perfect in our weakness!

People will probably forget what you say during a hard time, but they will never forget how you loved them through it.

One of the most important things to remember while ministering to the hurting is that you are not God. You may never be able to answer the "Why?" or "What do I do now?" questions. You may not know the full story and may never know what God is accomplishing through these events and the grief you and others are experiencing. Sometimes, you will have to trust that God is working everything for the good of those who love Him and are called to His purpose (see Romans 8:28). You can offer advice or even an opinion. Unfortunately, some of the time, it may be the wrong advice and, honestly, your opinion does not really matter to those who are grieving. Always remember that people will probably forget what you say during a hard time, but they will never forget how you loved them through it.

Please, Don't Wear the Sign!

When people are hurting, they need someone who is full of compassion and the presence of God. They do not need re-criminations. I have to be honest. Some of the things I have heard come out of people's mouths—including those of pastors and their wives—during a time of loss have completely floored me. Personally, I have learned to live by this mantra from Abraham Lincoln: "Better to remain silent and be thought a fool than to speak out and remove all doubt." Basically, if I don't know what to say, I just shut up! The last thing I need is to carry around the "Stupid Pastor's Wife" sign on my back.

So, with that preface, let me give you some things which can be very healing to those who are hurting, along with . . . well, some things which will merit you wearing the dreaded "stupid" sign on your back.

Good Things to Say to Those Who are Hurting

1. "I am so sorry this happened."
2. "I do not understand it either."
3. "I wish I could say something to take away the hurt."

4. "Can I take you out of the house for a while?"
5. "Let me take your children somewhere to play, so you can get some rest or regroup."
6. "Can I hold you in a tight hug for a few minutes?"
7. "Let me hold your baby for a while."

Some Really Stupid Things to Say

AFTER A DIVORCE:

1. "At least you didn't have any kids."
2. "I knew you would never make that marriage work."
3. "I told you so."
4. "You really are better off now."
5. "I have a really great friend I would like you to meet."

AFTER A MISCARRIAGE:

1. "At least you never felt the baby move."
2. "Thank God you didn't have to go through labor and delivery like I did."
3. "Lots of women miscarry."
4. "There must have been something wrong with the baby; it was probably retarded and this was God's way of protection."
5. "It's better this way."

CONCERNING BARRENNESS:

1. "God told me that you would have a baby by the end of this

year."

2. "Don't feel bad; lots of women can't have babies."
3. "Boy, would I like to give you mine!"
4. "Why don't you just work in the nursery? That will cure you."

CONCERNING DEATH:

1. "God just needed another angel." (Since when did souls convert to angelic creatures?)
2. "God will send you someone better next time."
3. "I want you to meet my grandson."
4. "There must have been some sin in his/her life."
5. "You just didn't have enough faith."
6. "Somebody spoke a curse over his/her life."
7. "You should have taken them to a better doctor."

DURING FINANCIAL DIFFICULTY:

1. "You should have planned better."
2. "God will help you use this in your testimony one day."
3. "Well, I saw it coming when you bought that new car."
4. "You can always get government assistance."
5. "I've got some old clothes I can give you if you need them."
6. "I'll pray that God will send someone to help you."
7. "This is what happens when you don't tithe."
8. "Bankruptcy isn't as bad as it used to be. Lots of people file nowadays."

Stay with What You Know

here are things firmly established in the Word of God. We do know God is good, His love for mankind is undying, and He knows what is best for us. We know our tragic situations do not take God by surprise to where He paces wringing His hands in worry saying, "Oops, I didn't see that one coming!" God saw it—and made provision for it.

Here are few other absolutes to help you process grief during times of loss.

1. **Bad things happen to good people.** This is not God's punishment. Remember, He took out His wrath toward mankind on Jesus on the cross over 2000 years ago!

   "Dear friends, do not be surprised at the painful trial you are suffering as though something strange were happening."

   1 PETER 4:12 (NIV)

2. **Pain and heartache is inevitable.** They will come. We live in a world full of pain; and God never promised to remove it, but rather to give us grace to walk through it.

   "God gives to us and He takes away from us. May the name of the Lord be praised."

   JOB 1:21 (NKJV)

3. There is an end to grief. Separation will not last forever.

"But I do not want you to be ignorant, brethren, concerning those who have fallen asleep, lest you sorrow as others who have no hope. For if we believe that Jesus died and rose again, even so God will bring with His, those who sleep in Jesus. For this we say to you by the word of the Lord, that we who are alive and remain until the coming of the Lord will by no means precede those who are asleep. For the Lord Himself will descend from heaven with the voice of the archangel, and with the trumpet of God and the dead in Christ will rise first. Then we who are alive and remain shall be caught up together with them in the clouds to meet the Lord in the air. And thus we shall always be with the Lord. Comfort one another with these words."

1 THESSALONIANS 4:13-18 (NKJV)

Two things can happen through a time of grief or pain: it can mold a person or define them. When people are molded, grief shapes the way they walk, the way they talk, and the way they respond. Being defined by grief is when their whole life is related to the amount of pain and heartache they have faced. Sadly, this becomes a reference point for the rest of their life. They will always be the "one who can't get pregnant," the "one whose daughter committed suicide," the "one whose wife abandoned him," or the "one who survived the car crash."

Think about Bartimaeus in the Bible. For centuries—even to this day—people have defined him by his affliction as "blind Bartimaeus." But the truth is, he didn't stay blind! Jesus miraculously healed him, and he went about proclaiming the goodness of God. So, why don't we call him "healed Bartimaeus?" It is simply because human nature defines people by the tragedy which has marked their life.

But, there is a better way. The reality is life hurts and people go through very unfortunate situations. The good news—better known as the Gospel—is that they do not have to stay in those circumstances nor live their lives under the banner of loss or defeat. As ministry families, we must be ready to help people through the initial time

* *

> *Two things can happen through a time of grief or pain: it can mold a person or define them.*

* *

of grief, but also be able to lead them to a point of recovery. Be ready. The depths of grief and the time for adequate healing will vary depending on each person's spiritual life and the gravity of their loss. The key to walking someone through grief is to walk *through* it, to be changed and molded *by* it, and to learn to truly trust God *in* it, that He does have a plan.

This is the better way—the God-kind of recovery!

Footnote:

"LIfes is short, wear cute shoes."

15

A Closet Full of Shoes

My darling husband, Randy, is like most men who think having large amounts of shoes is very confusing. He needs only one pair of each type of shoe: brown dress, black dress, burgundy dress, tennis, everyday, beach, and bedroom slippers. The only exception is for his golf shoes, of which he has three pairs! One pair is to wear on really nice, prestigious golf courses and for playing in tournaments, one is for muddy golf courses, and then he has his spare pair.

Having so many shoes in one closet can be quite overwhelming for the person who does not know or appreciate the purpose of each pair. To them, too many choices equal too much confusion. For years, I have tried my best to help Randy understand how different clothing requires a different style of shoes. For instance: a black pump may be needed for a black corporate suit, but a different heel height may be needed for a suit with a different length skirt. Functionality is also an issue. Sequined pumps are not going to cut it at the beach, while flip-flops just don't work with an evening gown.

After years of explanation and education, he still doesn't see how different styles call for different shoes. He cannot fathom why it should matter if one pair has a taller, thinner, or decorated heel, and the other does not. To him, they're all the same. If he needs a pair of black shoes, he just puts on his black shoes. End of story. He does not take the time—nor see the need—to choose between two or three different styles of black shoes. In fact, if he decides to buy a new pair of black shoes, he gets rid of the old black shoes. Not me. I may need the other pair for a different outfit. One of my shoe friends told me that she has ten pairs of black pumps. I am sure they all have a separate function. But, Randy just shakes his head in disbelief!

For your church to operate at its highest potential and reach its ultimate effectiveness, you must have the right person in the right ministry at the right time.

Trust me, a closet full of various shoes, styles, colors, and purposes can be very difficult to manage. It kind of resembles your church staff, doesn't it? An office full of various staff members with different backgrounds, responsibilities, educations, expectations, and experience. In the full scope of operating any church or organization, one of the key elements is to know the people with whom you are working; learning their strengths and weaknesses and giving them the freedom to operate in their areas of ministry without micro-managing their every move and decision. For your church to operate at its highest potential and reach its ultimate effectiveness, you must have the right person in the right ministry at the right time.

Sometimes, this is easier said than done.

Building Your Closet

*J*ust as every closet is different, every church is unique in their operations and structure. It's partly what makes you distinct and set apart. Knowing this, it is not my intention to show you how we are structured, so you can follow it exactly. Besides, it might not work even in your particular situation. However, whenever Randy and I were in the primary stages of building our ministry "closet of different shoes," some examples of working, functional staffs would have greatly helped us and saved us from some very costly mistakes. Hopefully, the next few pages and personal examples will be a good resource for you as you build the team God is placing in your church.

With our staff, each pastor has his own portfolio of ministry which clearly explains how and where he/she is to function and what issues he/she must manage. While they are busy doing the work within their particular ministry portfolios, they are all also part of a larger, broader ministry. We have found that when individual parts of the ministry function properly, it makes the whole ministry stay healthy.

I Have Issues

From Two to Seventeen——and Counting

Through the years of full-time ministry, my husband and I have had many different types of staff members. When we first began in youth ministry, we had a team of youth leaders, chaperones, and sponsors, all of who were non-paid volunteers. Most of these leaders had either just come through the youth ministry or were parents of a teenager. These people were such a blessing in many ways, but because they were volunteers, it was a bit difficult to fire them! Nevertheless, they all had standards and guidelines which had to be followed, if they were going to be in a leadership position. Volunteerism meant they didn't get paid, but it did not excuse them from the responsibility of living a higher standard of life, far above reproach.

We took some principles from our first youth ministry team of volunteers and have included them with all of our paid staff as well. For example: each ministry within the church should have clear guidelines for every leader to follow, regardless of the position held. The pastoral ministry is responsible to develop, implement, and reinforce these guidelines, along with administrating the proper discipline if not followed. All responsibilities, policies, and disciplines should be in writing and should be signed by all potential leadership team members. Various areas of ministry could have specific policies designed especially for that department.

For instance, single youth leaders may not be allowed to have a dating relationship with anyone currently in the youth program, or choir members may be required to attend a minimum amount of rehearsals each month. (NOTE: Every pastor should be aware of state and local laws regarding those who work with children. In our ministry, all paid staff *and* volunteers who work with children or youth must pass a criminal background records check.)

During our first pastorate, our staff included two people—me and Randy! Shortly after we had taken this position, a young man moved into our town and began volunteering at the church. One of his goals was to gain hands-on experience in the ministry. For many months, Randy mentored him, and we were eventually able to hire him as our full-time youth/associate pastor. We were so relieved! We now had our first staff member. While he was on our staff, the church grew, and we added more support and pastoral staff. We thought having three or four staff members was all God would allow us to manage. Boy, were we wrong!

In our current pastorate, we started with three full-time pastors and now have grown to more than 17! This does not include our support personnel, maintenance, janitorial, daycare, and school staff. Some of the pastoral staff have been with us more than 10 years, and others less than six months. Some have left of their own accord, while others were allowed to resign their positions. Then there were those who have been purposefully relieved of their duties. We have cried to see some leave, but knew it was time. For those who stayed too long, we danced as they left the building. And, on a few occasions, we have had to fight the urge of slamming the door in their face as they left. I remember one time when I asked Randy to leave me alone in a room with a particular staff member and a baseball bat. (I did have to ask Jesus to forgive me of that one.) Like any growing organization, we have definitely had the good, the bad, and the ugly.

Church growth always brings its fair share of difficulties. One of those is hiring pastoral staff. A senior pastor must be extremely careful when adding another leadership personality (and their issues) to a growing church. As our church in Griffin has grown, the body

of people in the church has been very accepting of new pastoral staff
and their families. I believe one of the reasons for this acceptance is
our current staff sets the example of acceptance to the church body.
We all make a positive, conscious effort to incorporate new staff into
current staff dynamics.

Getting to Know You

*E*very staff is a work in progress. There will always be some type
of transition occurring. Nailing down an entire staff on a permanent basis is kind of like nailing Jell-O® to a tree. It is impossible.
Some staff will be long-term; some will be transitional; and some will
be in training for their next assignment.

When we are in a position to hire new pastoral staff, we begin by
looking for specific qualities and characteristics in the individual *and* in their
family. During this time, we ask very deliberate questions to help facilitate
the interview process. The questions might be asked and answered verbally
or just through conversation. Some of these questions will be:

* Where is their spiritual walk? Are they more interested in
  money or in the will of God?

* Do they want to grow in their walk with God, and do they feel this
  can be accomplished at this church under this pastoral ministry?

* Are they qualified for the job? Are they capable of learning,
  or are we setting them up to fail?

* Will they fit into the current staff dynamics and be able to

interact with the current staff on a personal and professional level?

* Have they been too wounded to properly minister? Do they need a sabbatical before filling another ministry position?

* Why do they want to be a part of this staff? Why do they want to leave their current position?

* Do they feel called to this particular area and region?

* How will their spouse and children fit into the role?

* Will they be able to interact with other staff families, or will they hold themselves aloof?

* Do they know what it means to walk through pain and heartache and still be victorious?

* Do they have teachability, passion, and a good, strong work ethic?

While this list of questions is not completely comprehensive, it gives us a starting point in becoming acquainted with the potential pastor and his/her family. As you can tell, the family is a *definite* part of the process.

The New Kid in Town

*W*henever we hire a new staff member, we try to make the transition as easy as possible for all involved. Sometimes, churches need to grieve the loss of a staff member—either as they are preparing to leave or after they have departed. As senior pastors, we try to allow the church adequate time to grieve and then set the stage for the arrival of the new staff member. Inevitably, there will be comparisons made between the new and the old personalities, the former way of doing things, and the administrations of any new staff.

A few years ago, our music ministries began to really grow, and we realized the need for an assistant music pastor. With the increased people, ministries, and activities in the music department, our music pastor was carrying a very heavy load. The new assistant was responsible to help with the praise teams, ensembles, youth choir,

A pastor can set the atmosphere and the acceptance for change better than anyone else.

and to also develop a music track for our school of ministry. To prepare the people involved in the music ministry for the change, our music minister began telling people that we were getting ready for an opportunity of new growth. There would be some changes, but the Kingdom of God was about the overall good for the Body of Christ, not individual personalities. He also spoke about the acceptance of change and how nothing in life that is growing ever stays the same.

What a blessing this preparation was when our new assistant

came on staff. Those already involved in the music ministry were prepared for change. Sure, there were some minor ripple effects, but had our music minister not prepared the music department for those changes, the fallout would have been much worse. You see, a pastor can set the atmosphere and the acceptance for change better than anyone else.

The Dry Cleaners and the Bistro

*W*henever new staff members are added to your team, everybody experiences change: the church, the staff, and the new staff member. For their family, there will be a new home, new town, new doctors, different grocery and variety stores, unfamiliar roads, places to go and those to avoid, new directions, new schools, and other information which seems simple, but they are all things which most locals take for granted. On the work side of things, new staff will need to adapt to new procedures and guidelines and, at times, change their mode of operation or thought processes to make a smooth transition for the greater good.

When we first moved to Griffin, I had the chore of finding a new, good, dry cleaners. (Not every business that hangs a dry cleaning sign over their door actually does a good job!) I asked a few people for their recommendations, but information was sparse. While driving to the church one day, I noticed a building about a half mile down the road with a dry cleaner's sign. They had purposely spelled a word wrong in their name, and it caught my eye. I thought it was a cute way to advertise. Plus, it was the closest one to our house. So, I took a newly-made dress of bridal satin to them for spot cleaning and pressing. A few days later, I returned to pick up my dress only to find that it had been ruined. The sequins were burned into the fabric. Needless to say, I was very upset. When I called the owner, he cussed me out and blamed me for his mistake. I thought, "Wow, welcome to Griffin!" He never did resolve the problem, and I discovered later that he carried this same reputation all over town for this very thing. I guess I should have known better than to use a dry cleaner that misspelled their own name!

After we had lived here for a little while, I wanted to try a restaurant I found on the outskirts of town. It looked very inviting and promised to be a delicious meal. When I mentioned my intentions for lunch one day, a member of our church explained to me that it was in fact not a restaurant, but a "honky-tonk" (another way of saying it was a cheap bar.) Can you imagine my reaction if I would have walked in expecting a nice little bistro for lunch? I would have been mortified— much like my reaction when picking up my dress from the dry cleaners! Funny, this same bar is now named after a popular exercise studio for women, but it is a topless bar. One of our staff members inquired about this establishment and I, too inform them that it was not the new location of the fitness center, but a new twist on an old problem.

Transition is never easy; and as a senior pastor's wife, you can do some initial things to make it easier for a new staff family. Here are just a few things to incorporate.

1. **Make yourself available to answer any questions conce-rning geographical areas of your town.** I always try to explain at least the basic layout of our roads, even taking the wife with me on quick trips close to the church, so she can get her bearings. Even then, she may still get lost. This is why I stress the need for our staff members to have a cell phone programmed with all the staff's telephone numbers—preferably on speed dial!

2. **Assign a staff pastor to the incoming pastor and his family.** Include the current staff pastor's wife to be available for the new family. Have her to check and make sure the "settling in" process is proceeding well. Check to see that they have food to eat, a place to sleep, and any other help they might need. This assignment should be based within the area of ministry for the incoming pastor. For instance, the executive music pastor and his family will oversee the transition of the new assistant music pastor and his family. Always have a backup just in case the established pastor's wife should happen to be sick, out of town, or have something unexpected to handle. Have another staff lady assigned to help. Remember, most wives are not considered as staff members. Anything they do is volunteer and done out of their love for the ministry and for each other.

3. **Put together an informational booklet for incoming staff members.** This booklet can contain the telephone numbers and addresses for various home and personal needs: medical professionals, hospitals, good places to eat, delivery restaurants, hair dresser, nail shops, alterations, car repair, electricians, plumbers, handy men, and so on. Some of these professionals could already be a part of your church, while others are in the community. Ask current staff wives for recommendations on these and other necessary items. Do not publish any unpleasant or negative comments; just simply do not include those establishments or services.

4. **Produce a list of all pastoral staff names, telephone numbers, and e-mail addresses.** Include this in a "welcome packet" and deliver it upon their arrival. Then, update it as needed.

The First Wives Club

*M*inistry can be a very lonely life, especially for pastor's wives. On our staff, our pastors have the opportunity to connect with other staff members, ministers, or accountability partners; however, the same opportunity usually does not present itself to their spouses. Even if it did, some minister's wives would not participate, as they feel the need to hide their emotions from people in the church and often, even from other staff pastor's wives. They may be at home, drowning under the pressures of marriage, family, and ministry with no one to express how they are dealing with these issues.

I'm reminded of what Paul, the Apostle, said:

> *"We do not want you to be ignorant, brethren, of our trouble which came to us in Asia: that we were burdened beyond measure, above strength so that we despaired even of life."*

> 2 CORINTHIANS 1:8

The feeling of isolation is horrible. To combat this with our staff wives, I have tried to create an atmosphere where they can feel totally safe. They have a place where they can vent to other women without fear of repercussions. (Notice the use of the preposition "to," not "at.") To create this atmosphere, I have tried to become as spiritually and emotionally transparent as possible. This is not an easy task for me, since I am a very private person by nature. However, I have found the way to nurture healthy staff members is to offer a place where they can come to me in vulnerability, without fear, and know I will not think they are "crazy" or ungodly. This type of vulnerability can only be established once they see it modeled by me. Then, by mutual consent, we become open and less guarded with each other. We feel safe because we are connected.

One of the ladies in our church has labeled our staff wives as the "First Wives Club." I guess we do have our own little sorority, since we deal with issues which are not only related to life, but ministry life. (Many college sorority sisters stay connected for life, and this is what I desire from our staff wives. We all need the support system both now and for years to come.) Once a month, our First Wives Club meets for breakfast or dinner. Some of our staff wives work outside the home and cannot be available at all hours, so we try to be flexible. This setting is usually in a private room, or we have a meal catered. It is one of the ways we encourage openness and vulnerability. Our conversations are private and confidential.

During our meeting, we spend a lot of time catching up on in each other's lives. We also share personal and staff needs, discuss any issues we may be facing, and have a time of prayer together. Concerning church business and activities, I usually give each one present a list of important dates which covers the upcoming three months. I will update the list each subsequent month. For major events, the staff wife most connected with the event will take some time to explain the details and how each person can help. For example, on October 31, we celebrate Harvest Night. This event is designed with children in mind, but adults are needed in masses to make this evening happen. The children's pastor hosts this event, so during our meeting a month prior, his wife will share the details and inform us of any outstanding items which need our help or attention. Even though it is children's department function, we all pitch in to ensure its maximum success.

Even though monthly meetings help us to stay informed,

day-to-day issues sometimes sneak up on us. To help forestall issues, I have set a few guidelines in place which are given to each staff wife when they become a part of our team. Occasionally, I reiterate these guidelines in our monthly meetings. Should a conflict or an issue arise, my first reference is to these guidelines to help solve the problem. I also challenge the wives to do check this list as well:

1. **This is a family.** We are the only family you have in this entire place. You are my brother, my sister. My children are also part of your family. If you see them do something good, tell them—and me—about it. The same if you see them do something wrong. My children and your children are brothers and sisters. They will argue. There will be sibling rivalry. But, we will all nurture them together. I will hug your children, love them intensely, spoil them, and give them candy when you are not looking. I will not let anyone say your children are brats, even if their behavior is deserving of the indictment. We all live in a fishbowl, but I am the Mama Barracuda, and I will not hesitate to bite anyone who comes after me or mine. We are here to help one another be more effective in winning the world for Christ. We cannot accomplish our mission if we are not in unity. I need your help. We are family.

2. **If you need help, ask for it.** If I cannot help you, I will find someone who can. If you are sick and cannot take care of yourself, we will be there to help you clean your house, prepare a meal, or take your children for the afternoon. If we cannot do it, we will try to find someone who can. But this is not a free ride. When you recover, you may be required to do the same thing for one of your sisters.

When you have a baby, we will bring meals for one week. If you need more, just tell me. Remember, you knew for months that this day was coming. Hopefully, you prepared for days of being unable to cook and unable to think past breastfeeding or dirty diapers. If you tell me you need extra help and I don't agree, I may tell you. You may need to grow up and learn how to be responsible. If you think you don't need help but it's obvious you do, I may tell you or show up at your house with a "Help You Committee." There is no need for you to go to an early grave just because you were too proud to ask for help. Your husband will only remarry, and someone else will get your wedding china! Then we'll have to train someone else to take your place.

3. **Do not receive accusations against another staff member.** If you haven't noticed, women are known to be gossipers; but Christian women often label their gossip as "prayer requests." It doesn't really matter what label you put on it. If you have something to say, do it in front of the person involved or don't say it at all.

4. **Do not try to answer an offense for another staff member.** In the quest for transparency, oftentimes the congregation may think this gives them the freedom to complain about other staff members. I don't address complaints and expect other staff wives to follow suit. Let them run their course and forget about them. Learn to recognize the difference between a complaint and a true offense. If you were not present when the offense occurred and do not know the circumstances surrounding it, then

you are not equipped to answer it. To do so would be mere speculation and possibly cause more offense. If anyone hears that someone has taken offense with one of our staff members—correctly or incorrectly—the staff member involved is responsible for their own words and actions and must handle it.

I have found that one of the best ways to handle an offense is to "plead the fifth" if you are ignorant of the root reason. For example, if during a music production, one of our staff wives changed the staging position of another staff wife, this might be misconstrued by other choir members and lead to an offense. Maybe she perceives there are deeper issues at hand rather than a simple misplacement. After vocalizing her offense to another person, it can grow exponentially. Upon hearing this mishap, offended members need to be addressed and told the facts, nipping in the bud any chance for hurt or disillusionment. Make it your priority to restore unity at any cost.

5. **You may be trusted with highly confidential information.** Never forget what the phrase "highly confidential" means: you share it with no one! If you feel the need to unburden yourself, do it with someone else whom you are confident has privy to the same information. Breaking confidentiality could result in the loss of trust . . . or position. There could also be legal ramifications. Many times, you are perceived as an extension of your spouse, thus the same legal rules should apply to you in the area of confidentiality.

6. **Find your confidante among other staff members, not church members.** When Elijah was running from

Jezebel, he felt as though he was the only one who was living wholeheartedly for God. In fact, Elijah had a really nice pity party with only three attendees—himself, the angel of the Lord, and a worm. The worm eventually ate him out of house and home.

Do not fall into the "Elijah Syndrome"—alienating yourself by resisting connection with anyone. Find someone with whom you can talk to who will listen and hold you accountable. There will be times when you wonder if what you do is really worth the sacrifices. We all go through those times of reflection. The key to getting up and moving forward is in allowing the Lord to restore you with food, water, and rest.

The value in having a confidante is priceless; however, in the ministry, you must be careful to not cross the boundaries between church members and staff. Many people in the church do not understand the pressures and the call of God on our lives, regardless of how much they may assure you of their understanding. Having a confidante from within the church body is running the risk of breaking a confidence and also possibly bringing disillusionment into their spiritual lives. It is never worth it.

7. **You never have the luxury of giving anyone a "piece of your mind."** As pastoral staff members, we answer to a higher call and a different set of rules. Even when you are wronged and have every right to let the person know how you feel, consider the reaction that is most prudent. Your testimony is more important than being right. Someone involved in your area of ministry may be connected to the person you have

just blasted with your words. Remember 1 Corinthians 13:6 which says love never takes into account a wrong suffered. This goes beyond the boundaries of marriage and the church world; it also includes how we present ourselves and our Savior to a lost and dying world.

When you are wronged, acknowledge it has happened and let the people involved know you are aware of it. If the problem can be resolved, then use all avenues available to you for resolution. If you cannot resolve the issue, put it on Jesus' account and let Him keep the books.

The Money Pit

Randy and I are strong believers in modeling what we expect from our staff. Ever so often, I tell our staff wives this story to remind them how important it is to keep a perspective of how we represent Jesus, not just the ministry.

A few years ago, Randy and I purchased a home in our town from a local builder. Although he had lived in it for six or eight weeks, he gave us a full, one-year warranty. Within days of moving in, we began to have problems. Every toilet and sink leaked. Light fixtures shorted out. The yard drainage was poor and quickly resulted in erosion. The worst problem was the first time it rained, our roof leaked so badly that the water drained through an upstairs closet, all the way down through the floor and onto the ceiling of our master bedroom. To make matters even worse, the builder refused to do anything about the roof leak or the myriad of other problems we had already faced, and we had only been in the house for eight weeks!

After a calamity of errors, the Christian builder informed us that if we were unhappy, we should sue him. We tried to contact his home church and pastor all to no avail. He blocked all of our phone calls and refused to discuss the issue any further. So, we had a choice to make. We could, in fact, sue our "brother in Christ," or just let it go. We were definitely wronged and had a good legal case to pursue. But our testimony was more important to us than any rights we felt were due to us. With that conviction in mind, we chose to let it go. The home wound up costing us a lot of money for repairs—money we did not have at the time. However, we had to remind ourselves that Jesus keeps all accounts, not us.

To this day, we have never been able to rectify the problem with the builder, but we can stand before him and the throne of God knowing we did the right thing. We never vented our emotions nor gave him a "piece of our minds." Quite honestly, during this trial, we did not have any of our minds to spare!

Clean Out the Closet and Let it Go!

There are times when pastoral staffs change. Sometimes, we do not have to like it, but we do have to accept it. Change brings the opportunity to sharpen and stretch our own abilities along with the abilities of our staff members. We have come to realize that regardless of how much we love someone, we cannot keep them forever. To do so would possibly stunt their growth in the things God has for them. We have to accept whatever is the best for the individual, their family, the church, and the Kingdom.

Whenever a staff member leaves our church, it can fall into one of two categories: they have resigned or they have been fired. It is that simple. Each scenario brings a different perspective and a different set of circumstances.

RESIGNATION

Someone once said that a good family will either self-destruct or it divides and rebuilds. A good, natural family will not remain the same. Some new members will be introduced, while others will leave. Life and death demand changes. Because our staff is a ministry family, we, too must also learn how to divide and rebuild. We are continually making disciples and training others for leadership responsibilities. When the opportunity arises for them to begin practicing what they have learned, we must allow them to follow the opportunity and use what they have learned to further the Kingdom of God. As well-intended as this sounds, it is rarely easy.

We have also learned that we must give them wings to fly—even when we think they are not ready. Who knows? We could be wrong. Only they and God can determine what God's ultimate plan is for their lives. We can be available to mentor, call, check on their progress, and catch them if they fall; but we cannot hold onto them forever.

RELEASED

Whenever a person is fired from our staff, it never comes as a surprise to them. We all knew the day was coming, and usually it is the result of a series of misdeeds and written warnings. Although it has been rare, when a staff member has been terminated, one of the best things we have learned to do is to just let them go. They may need to know that you are available for spiritual support. In offering this support, it is important to not cross the line and begin to replace the importance of couple support. Couples need to believe in each other's own spiritual life and their family unit. Do not cross that boundary.

As hard as it may be at the moment, exposing sin can be the best thing to happen in a person's life, and in a minister's life. Always do what is right, not what is popular. When you have sin within your staff and it is exposed, allow time for healing and restoration both for the staff member, the remaining staff, and the church in general. Giving the departed staff member a good recommendation for another ministry position too quickly can prove to be spiritual and ministerial suicide. Allow them time to heal and be restored.

Wounded emotions take time to heal. It may be years before you can freely converse with the person you have had to terminate. Honestly, it may never ever happen. You may have no ill will against your former staff member, but they may never see past the trauma of their termination. On the other hand, they possibly could someday thank you for pushing them to change their behavior or work performance.

As a leader, keep your hand extended. It may not be easy, but find the strength to do it.

> *"But if any has caused sorrow, he has caused sorrow not to me, but in some degree—in order not to say too much—to all of you. Sufficient for such a one is this punishment which was inflicted by the majority, so that on the contrary you should rather forgive and comfort him, lest somehow such a one be overwhelmed by excessive sorrow. Wherefore I urge you to reaffirm your love for him."*

2 Corinthians 2:5-8 (NASB)

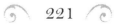

Regardless of the place you may be in staffing your team, many considerations must be made. Issues always occur with multiple staff members who have various personalities, ideas, needs, levels of leadership and spiritual maturity, and different ethnic and cultural backgrounds. Weaving all of these issues together takes someone with a desire to make it happen plus a lot of work and a definite plan of action. Multiple staffs never just "happen on accident." When every staff member realizes they are all on the same team, serving together, and enjoying what God is doing in the ministry, they begin to operate in unity and in one accord.

Just as every shoe in my closet has a specific purpose, so does every staff member. Using my shoes, or staff members, for something they were not designed to do would cause havoc and serious frustration in the wardrobe of this ministry. However, giving staff the freedom to do the jobs they were destined to do, results in contented and devoted people who truly desire to be used by God for the good of His Kingdom.

Footnote:

"A lie can travel halfway around the world while the truth
is still putting on its shoes."

Mark Twain

16

Color Steps—Not Quite Right

MY ISSUE: *SIN IN THE BODY OF CHRIST*

*I*n the 1980's, a new product specifically designed for coloring shoes was introduced called Color Steps®. It was an easy process: you just mixed the necessary combination of paints and then apply it to your shoes. It was fabulous for making an old pair of shoes look new or giving a current pair in the closet a facelift. There was only one problem with this revolutionary product: the paint was color-fast once it dried; but in matter of days, it became very easy to scrape off. You might have found yourself with new color on your shoes, but remnants of the old color were seen on the heel where the paint had lifted. After using this product, I really believe spray paint might have worked better, but I just didn't think about it at the time.

I once had a beautiful teal suit that needed beautiful shoes to match. (What's the use of having a great suit without the shoes, right?) After searching through many stores and catalogs for the exact match, I saw the advertisement for Color Steps® on television. "Ah, how perfect," I thought, "I can just paint an older pair to match." I purchased the necessary paints needed for my desired color and began the process of mixing and painting, mixing and painting, and mixing and painting some more in order to find just the perfect shade of teal. After hours of what felt like a college chemistry lab assignment, I had it! I painted the shoes, waited for them to dry, and then sealed the paint. Finally, my search for the perfect match for my suit was over.

The next Sunday morning, I donned my teal suit and matching shoes and headed off to church. As soon as I walked into the doors of the church, a certain smart-aleck (who shall remain nameless) passed me and said, "I hope you don't think those shoes really match that suit." I began to look at them in the sunlight and realized they really did not match at all. They looked perfect at my house and in the car, but it was only after I stood in the sun that I realized the color was drastically wrong. Because I had looked at them so much during the painting process, I lost perspective of what color they really needed to be. I was way off, but it took the sunlight to disclose my mistake.

The Most Unpopular Word

There is an issue in life, much like my Color Steps® experience, which is not the most popular—or politically correct—term to use nowadays; but nevertheless, it is as real as the air you breathe. This issue, my friend, is called sin. Oftentimes, people think the things they are doing are really not that bad; when in reality, they have grown too familiar with it or do not see it in the correct light. Imperfections are only exposed in the true light—the light of the Holy Spirit. Not only does His light help us to see where we have sinned, but it also reveals the wrongs we have grown accustomed to doing. Along with the help of Holy Spirit, we all need the eye of another person—like an accountability partner—to expose the true color of what is in our lives. Sometimes that exposure will be private. However, if we still don't see it, then the exposure will become public.

There is an issue in life which is not the most popular nowadays.

So, let's take a minute and look at some areas to help recognize and remove any and all sin which might be lingering around just waiting for the right moment to bring calamity and chaos into your life and ministry.

1. **Sin is like an easy chair.** Have you ever noticed how your favorite easy chair is so easy to get into and so hard to get out of? Sin operates in the exact same manner. As you ease into it, its grasp becomes very comfortable; and before you even

realize it, you are in too far to get out. The cushions feel so good to your aching soul. Someone might even say that you deserve to be in this place and that it suits you better than anything else. You may not even realize how it has taken you to a place of ease, comfort, and deception until you are fast asleep in its arms.

2. **Sin has a formula.** Someone once said that sin will take you farther than you meant to go, cost you more than you are willing to pay, and keep you longer than you meant to stay. Oh, how true it is! It may start as a little thing which seems harmless and not a big deal, but the deception is that sin never lets you stay in one place of sinfulness. It leads you through a progression of self-lies (you know, the little white lies which lead to another and then yet another) until you find yourself addicted to the sin. You never intended to have an affair; it was only innocent flirting. You never intended to mortgage your house in order to keep your secret. You never intended for years to pass before really dealing with the root issue. No one ever intended for anyone to get hurt and for it

Sin will take you farther than you meant to go, cost you more than you are willing to pay, and keep you longer than you want to stay.

to end this way—no one, except the devil.

3. **When temptation comes calling, hang up. Don't wrestle with temptation and try to make excuse**s as to why it isn't really that bad. You will lose that fight and cause heartache to many people. Joseph, the son of Jacob, gave the best illustration of how to properly handle temptation: RUN! Even if you have to leave part of your clothing behind, just run as fast as you can. Don't entertain the idea and then try to justify yourself out of the temptation. You cannot resist it alone, so run from it as far away as possible.

I heard a little voice whisper in my head, "Go ahead, Jelly. Pull the lever. No one will ever know."

I will never forget the day I was faced with a strong temptation to gamble. Our family was vacationing at a resort in the Bahamas and on this particular day, everyone was at the beach, so I decided to stroll through the hotel lobbies. Wouldn't you know it, the only way to get from one section of the hotel to another was through the casino! It is such a beautiful room with opulent décor. Up until this particular moment, I can truthfully say I had never gambled nor ever sensed the desire to do so. Passing the slot machines, I heard a little voice whisper in my head, "Go ahead, Jelly. Just think, you could pay for your entire family vacation with one pull of the lever. No one will ever know. No one will ever know." Immediately, another voice broke into my thoughts and screamed, "I WOULD KNOW!" I knew it was God speaking to me, so I found the closest exit and exited as fast as possible. For the rest of our trip—and to this day—I have never walked through a casino alone again. I want to protect myself against any temptation and not wrestle or argue with it. If I must run, then I will run and let God be my rear guard!

> *"Guard my life, for I am devoted to you. You are my God; save your servant who trusts in you."*

PSALM 86:2

4. **Starve sin, and it will die.** I had a wonderful professor in college who made this classic statement to all of his classes on a regular basis. Professor Crandall Miller said, "What you feed grows, and what you starve dies." It took a few years for me to understand the whole truth of what he was saying. I knew that eating too much junk food and not exercising would make me grow more than I had intended. Of course, it could also kill me, as well. It was years later before I began to apply this principle to my spiritual life. I found that by feeding my spiritual life with God-li-ness, my God-like-ness would grow. If I didn't, then my spirit would shrivel and die from improper nourishment. In the same manner, feeding sinfulness into my life would generate a stronger desire for

sinful things. It would eventually overtake any sense of righteousness in my life and dominate my mind and actions. The key was simple: whenever I began to starve the sin, it began to die.

. . . .

I found that by feeding my spiritual life with God-li-ness, my God-like-ness would grow.

. . . .

5. **Sometimes doing the right thing causes pain.** In the Old Testament, there are many things which occurred in battles that make no sense to us, like killing babies. For the longest time, I never understood why God gave the command to kill all the Amalekite babies in one battle. When I learned that "Amalekite" was a type of sin, I then understood the significance of killing their babies. You see, little Amalekites grew up to be big Amalekites, and it was harder to kill the adult Amalekites than the babies.

Let me make one thing extremely clear: in no way, shape, form, or fashion am I saying or even suggesting that someone today has the God-given right to end their child's life prematurely. The Amalekites had no hope for salvation because they were not God's chosen people. The practice of killing their young is nothing more than an example of how we, today, should destroy sinfulness in our lives at its infant stage. If we do this, then sin never becomes fully grown, possessing the ability to rule our lives and destroy the things we love. Little sins are just as dangerous as big sins—they both lead to death.

First Things First

As Christian leaders, we are required to battle not only the sinfulness in our own lives, but also in our churches and/or other places where we lead. Sin—not politics, people, or militias—is what destroys churches, ministries, people, and cultures. Even though destruction is manifested through various means, the root is the evil one: Satan. He is sin, personified.

As ministers, we must first battle sin in our own lives, then our homes, relationships, and ministries. We simply take care of our own sinfulness—getting the proverbial beam out of our own eye—and then deal with the issue of external sin. It is impossible to bring holiness to a congregation if the leadership is unholy.

There are many examples in God's Word of how leadership sinned. Just read the stories of Eli and his sons, King David and his sons, Samson, Saul, Ananias and Sapphira, the early church, and the churches in the book of Revelation. These are real people in real situations who offer tremendous insight of what to do and more importantly, what *not* to do.

When I began my Christian life in earnest, there were certain things I did not participate in because God's Word declared it as SIN. I had no real problem with it. Even though I was a free thinker and wanted to do my own thing, I had a deep respect for God and wanted to please Him with my actions. So, things considered "big sins" were not my issue. It was what I viewed as the little things in life that really threw me: unforgiveness, envy, jealousy, etcetera. In other words, I could avoid breaking the Big Ten (commandments), but the "shadowy sins" could easily become my constant companion. Before I knew it, I found myself with bad attitudes which produced bad actions. My vine of life was definitely being destroyed by the "little foxes" nibbling away at my character.

Throughout my life, I found that unfaithfulness to God brings unrighteous thoughts, which then lead to sin. My faithfulness to God has to first be established in my heart and then demonstrated in my life. For the beginning of our ministry, I determined that my own personal, spiritual life would come *first*, and my ministry life would be birthed from my relationship with God. The ministry could

Unfaithfulness to God brings unrighteous thoughts, which then lead to sin.

never be the reason for my faithfulness to God. Over the years, this commitment has not been easy to sustain, so I have often referred to Psalm 85:10-13 for strength to keep my focus and priorities in order.

"Love and faithfulness meet together; righteousness and

> *peace kiss each other. Faithfulness springs forth from the earth, and righteousness looks down from heaven. The Lord will indeed give what is good, and our land will yield its harvest. Righteousness goes before him and prepares the way for his steps."*

Setting the Course

We face a crisis in ministry today in the fact that even if God's Word declares something to be "sin," we cannot be assured others will view it as such. Therefore, it is critically important to know God's Word, believe it in its entirety, and declare it to be infallible. Here are a few tips to help set your course in battling the subject of sin.

* **Establish your belief system.** This is one of the first things you must do in public ministry. Once this is created in your personal life first and the ministry secondarily, then you have a platform on which to stand. If you cannot declare God's Word to be true and infallible, then you have no platform or basis for your value system. You will find yourself surrounded by opportunity for situational ethics and are limited by the ability to base your life decisions on the circumstances of the moment. Personally, I have chosen to base my life on God's Word in its entirety; even if, at times, it is unpleasant, painful, or not the popular vote.

* **Live by your established, governing values.** Don't compromise. Don't sway. Don't mistakenly think the rules apply to everyone else except you and your family. Although you may be in ministry, God still requires that **you** follow the rules.

* **Decide on your battle plan.** If you have not established a Biblically-based value system or have not put it into practice, then you are not equipped to decide on a plan of action against the subject of sin. It doesn't really matter which shoes you are wearing at this point—mismatched, baby's, pastor's wife, or house shoes—or what issues you have in life, your steps must take the path and the plan of God's Word. When everything is in place, the battle plan will be laid out for you in precise order by the Spirit of God. Remember, the Bible only promises that the steps of a righteous man are ordered by the Lord.[1] There is no indication that the unrighteous can depend on God for clear direction.

* **Put on the armor of God.** Be ready to fight and go to battle. Lives and eternities hang in the balance. We are mandated by God to walk in the power of His Spirit and not yield to the flesh.

Facing the Inevitable

Mark my words: you will be faced with a sin problem in some form or fashion. It could be blatant sin or some sins of the

---

1   Psalms 37:23

heart yet to be publically exposed. Factually, this issue could manifest in issues which some do not even consider sin. If you have laid the ground work and properly set your course for battling sin, then you are ready for battle. Here is a good battle plan:

1. **Put a name on sin.** Too many ministers today have not followed the "proper procedure" for battling sin; and when

· ·

You will be faced with a sin problem in some form or fashion.

· ·

they meet it face-to-face within their churches, there is no plan of action. They possibly may have lived unrighteous themselves, thus cannot expose the sin in anyone else due to the high risk of self-exposure. If you are going to deal with sin in the church, you must be two things: righteous and courageous. Don't be afraid to talk about sinfulness. Call it what it is—S.I.N.—but live free of it yourself lest you become a casualty of your own message. Remember 1 Corinthians 9:27 which says:

> *"No, I beat my body and make it my slave so that after I have preached to others, I myself will not be disqualified for the prize."*

2. **Identify your enemy.** How can you battle something which you cannot identify? Randy and I had to do exactly this while considering our move to Griffin. Many ministers advised us not to relocate here. Some even said it would be a horrible mistake and a setback for our ministry. Their reasoning was that the church here had a long history of adulterous relationships which had destroyed many ministers and their families. One well-known pastor and several succeeding pastoral staff members had been plagued with infidelity and immorality. We heard their warnings, but knew we had received the Word of the Lord. For us to be in the perfect will of God, relocating to Griffin was not an option.

Within our first year of ministry in Griffin, we had to deal with the sin of adultery within our pastoral staff. The warnings of those who had spoken to us before prior to our move became daunting, but we quickly went to the Lord and received the revelation we needed. See, the root problem was not just in our church; the spirit of adultery was ruling our entire town! We found it to be an issue in many other churches in our city, as well. Everyone was fighting the same battle. As a community of churches, we began to bind together in prayer and fasting to battle this wicked spirit. I would never be so arrogant as to say the battle is over, but we have had many victories, and the enemy has been put to flight.

3. **Allow the sinner private repentance.** Luke 17:3 says, "If your brother sins, rebuke him; and if he repents, forgive him." Just be sure there is *true repentance* and not just remorse because of the impending embarrassment their sin will bring if

exposed. There should be evidence of repentance, including submission and humility. Now, this also does not mean that you put a thief in charge of counting the offering or a child molester in charge of the nursery. That goes without saying.

4. **Public sin may require public exposure.** There are times when sin begins very privately, but escalates to the public arena. For instance, Internet pornography may be something initially confined within someone's home. However, over the course of time, pornography is a sin of diminishing returns, requiring more and more stimulation. Those involved rarely keep it confined to the privacy of their own home. It may result in visits to strip clubs, prostitutes, or other kinds of adultery. When others become involved, the sin is then not just against one person; it is a sin against their family and also the Body of Christ. This type of public sin—especially if it occurs within your church leadership—must be dealt with in a public fashion, using as much humility and grace as possible. Letting it go with no explanation will corrupt the whole body.

5. **Provide true restoration for the repented heart.** One of the marks of true repentance is when the person is willing to do whatever is necessary to bring restoration. Give this person a detailed plan to regain trust and a place in your ministry leadership. This produces a hope and your genuine desire for reconciliation.

   One important key is to establish hedges of accountability, so they can protect themselves from future failure. Accountability is not designed for someone to control someone else's life. On the contrary, it is a network for people to receive Godly counsel, support, and the ability for someone to face their weaknesses and propensity to sin. Accountability is not to provide fodder for gossip, but rather provide a hedge of security set in place to thwart the onslaught of Satan toward one's weaknesses.

Footnote:

"One shoe can change your life."

Cinderella

17

Footjoy

MY ISSUE: *CHOOSING TO DANCE*

I have a dream. It may never come to pass; but even still, I have a dream. We have this ongoing discussion in our home about dancing and why we don't go to dances. Now, before you start sending me e-mails trying to convince me it is alright for our children to go to dances, don't. I will never believe it. Why? Because I believe dancing is a "vertical expression of a horizontal desire." (If you know what I mean!) What you believe is between you and God. I just do not want any man putting his hands on my girls, or touching his body to hers, unless they are married and then only in private. Then, they can decide what they want to do.

What does that have to do with my dream? Everything! I do enjoy watching some cultural dances and have a desire to learn some of them—not for church services, of course, but just for me. I am not talking about the hula dance, the tango, dirty dancing, or belly dancing (My belly already dances enough, thank you very much!). No, I have a dream to learn clogging! My husband thinks I'm crazy, and it's just my Tennessee roots coming out, among other things. For those of you who don't know what clogging is, let me explain it to you. Basically, it's a mixture of tap dancing in ruffles to hoe-down music. The ruffles aren't really what I like, nor the music; it's the shoes! They are usually shiny, black slippers with taps on the bottoms. Wherever you step, you hear a rattle-ching-tap over and over. The harder you step or stomp, the louder the noise. You certainly cannot sneak up on anyone while wearing these shoes, but it does make nice announcement that you are on your way.

Clogging is almost like watching pure joy in the feet. You cannot help but smile when you see all those legs, shoes, and ruffles flying around. I think God probably smiles, too. Who would have ever thought He could make feet that could move like that? It's amazing! Maybe even if I never do learn to clog, I can just get a pair of clogging shoes. This way, whenever I need to smile or laugh out loud, I could just put on my dancing shoes and go for it. It would be like choosing to smile, choosing to laugh, and choosing joy. It makes me think of Psalms 84:4 which says:

> *"Blessed are those who dwell in Your house; they will still be praising You."*

I say, "Bring on the clogging shoes, baby, and let the dancing begin!"

Pressure Release

As we live our lives, we find out how different circumstances often change us—some for the good, others not so good.

People will inevitably have an effect on our lives. Ministry will mold the ways we think and react. Disillusionment will appear in unexpected places.

As women in the ministry, we are made of strong fiber, but we are not invincible. We expect more from ourselves than we expect of other people and more than other people expect of us. At times, all of the tasks and demands are overwhelming, and we might be misunderstood. But guess what? You cannot do it all, but you can do what you can. Face it. Everyday pressures are real, not to mention the pressures of ministry to boot. So, how do you cope with day-to-day pressures? I am so glad you asked.

You dance!

1. **Get real.** Be yourself, not someone else. You have your own identity not necessarily based in motherhood or being a wife.

2. **See pressure for what it is.** Your particular circumstance can be the worst thing or the best thing that has ever come your way. Either way, make it fun.

3. **Take responsibility for your own joy.** Happiness is external and fleeting. Joy comes from your spirit, is not moved by

How do you cope with day-to-day pressures? You dance!

external surroundings, and is eternal. Find your joy!

4. **Harness the power of enthusiasm.** Get excited over the little things. Wipe mundane and cynical things out of your life. Habakkuk 3:17-18 says that even though there is no fruit on your vines and when your fields are producing no food, still rejoice in the Lord and joy in the God of your salvation!

5. **Follow the birds!** A bird does not sing because it has a song; it sings because it has a voice. You may feel as though there is nothing to be happy and joyful about, and that life will never get any better. Always remind yourself that you are a person who does not base her life on thoughts and feelings. Thoughts and feelings will come and go like the wind. Base your life on the Word of God, regardless of the circumstances. Simply praise God, not because you have song, but because you the ability to.

. . . .

A bird does not sing because it has a song; it sings because it has a voice.

. . . .

6. **Find one thing to laugh about everyday.** Some days you may have to look really hard, but it is there. Be creative. Find it.

7. **Guard yourself.** This is true especially in the books you read, the things you watch on television, and the people whom you spend time with. These three elements will play a major part in determining the person you become for many years. For example, if you are going through an attack of true, spiritual warfare in your home, don't read novels about the attacks of Satan on a minister's home. If an elderly loved one has recently died, don't watch a movie about old women who live alone and have no friends. Guard yourself and use wisdom.

8. **Stay positive even in a negative environment.** If you're not happy in your current place of ministry, try to find the positive in any situation. When Randy and I found ourselves in places where we felt more burden than breakthrough, we use to play a game called "The Glad Game." Here are a few scenarios:

   * You used bug spray instead of furniture polish. Be glad you won't have any bugs on your furniture.

   * You wrecked the church van. Be glad no one was with you when you did.

   * Your child put marshmallows in the clothes dryer. Be glad it wasn't the cat!

Someone once said, "Life is hard, but God is good." What a true statement! Life, in fact, is full of difficult tasks, disappointments, heartache, and pain. Regardless of your daily work, whether it is the ministry or other responsibilities, there will be days you would rather

. . . .

Life is hard, but God is good.

. . . .

not remember. But, there will also be good days; ones you would love to re-live again and again. Learn to focus on the good and not on the bad, to be positive in a negative situation. Re-training your thought processes to think on the positive will develop a tendency for you to remember the good things and not dwell on the bad. Keeping your mind on the good things enables you to go the distance and finish your race in life. Refuse to give up!

David's Story

I met David when we first moved to Griffin many years ago. The first time I remember seeing him, he was standing at the back of the church worshipping the Lord with all his might. He was so jubilant and demonstrative in his praise that I could not help but be somewhat envious. He was worshipping God with his whole body: arms, hands, feet, head, and mouth. David was totally tuned in to Jesus. I noticed that it never mattered who might be watching him or what others might have thought about his worship to the Lord. Nothing or no one was going to stop him! Every few moments, he would put something in his mouth and prance around like he was playing an instrument. I later discovered that David actually *was* playing an instrument. He would sneak a kazoo into his pocket before church and was playing along with the worship music!

What made his uninhibited worship to God even more special

was the fact that David has Down's Syndrome. In all of the years he has been at the church, he has never used his condition as a handicap. Actually, quite the opposite.

As I became more acquainted with David, I discovered his love for Jesus, Sunday school, and donuts. I'm not so sure which he loves the most: Sunday school because they serve donuts, or Sunday school on its own. I would lean to believe he loves the donuts more as I have watched him take extra donuts on Sunday morning, stash them in his pockets, and keep them until Sunday night, just in case he should get hungry. And he always does! (I say that with the biggest smile in my heart!)

Another one of David's loves is for the Special Olympics. He participates in every event he hears about and has won many ribbons and medals through the years. David's specialty is running. He is not as fast

As I became more acquainted with David, I discovered his love for Jesus, Sunday school, and donuts.

as some, but he has stamina. During one event a few years ago, David and his friends were in a race when he slipped and fell. His arms could not support his weight, and he fell face-first into the dirt. While he lay there, David had a decision to make. He could get up and finish the race, or he could lay there until someone came and helped him up. It really was not a difficult decision for David as he got up very quickly and continued the race. All of his friends were waiting at the finish line when David pulled himself up and started to run again.

The crowd went wild. David ran and ran as the crowd cheered. The louder they cheered, the faster he ran, determined to finish. He crossed the finish line, in much pain, to the cheers of the crowd and numerous "high fives" from his friends who were waiting. After the race had concluded and his friends and the crowd had gone away, David's parents discovered he had actually broken both arms in his attempt to break his fall. But he never quit! What an amazing example of finishing well!

Whenever life gets hard, I reflect on David and his broken arms. I think to myself, "If David can finish a race with two broken arms, then surely I, too can finish this ministry race." I may not have a blue ribbon waiting on me at the end of Sunday services or a crowd cheering me on to victory. I may run with broken arms and a broken heart, and may not see my friends on the sidelines cheering me on. There may not be a trophy in my home telling me what a winner I am. But in the long run, my trophies and winner's ribbons are displayed in the lives of those who have been changed, and the disciples who have made an impact for the cause of Christ. So why should I quit? Why give up? The finish line is so close, and I want to finish strong. I want to be found faithful and want for my life to count in this life and the afterlife.

Dance Until the End

Years ago, I made the decision that one day I was going to be a happy old lady, not a bitter, dried up, joyless old coot! It was a choice to dance all the way to the end. Just as I chose to re-program my thoughts to dwell on the positive, I also chose joy. Joy is not an emotion; it is a place. The words from Paul, the apostle, began to sink into my spirit: think about the things which are good, virtuous, just, honest, and of a good report.[2] It was then that I truly started to live as an overcomer.

* *

It was a choice to dance all the way to the end.

* *

Negative thoughts produce a negative quality in our lives. You don't have to be joyful in this life, but why not choose joy? Ask yourself, "What do I want to be when I grow old? What will be read at my eulogy and engraved on my tombstone?" For me, I would like for my epitaph to say, "We couldn't stop her dancing! We couldn't stop her joy! She danced all the way to Heaven!"

> *"Therefore do not cast away your confidence, which has great reward. For you have need of endurance, so that after you have done the will of God, you may receive the promise."*

> **HEBREWS 10:35-36 (NKJV)**

---

2 Philippians 4:8, 9

I Have Issues

In 2000, country music superstar Martina McBride recorded a song which quickly became one of my favorites. I believe, as the conclusion of this book, there would not be a more appropriate message than this: whatever comes your way, choose to love, choose to rejoice, choose to dream, choose to dance—and dance all the way until the end!

I hope you never lose your sense of wonder,
You get your fill to eat but always keep that hunger,
May you never take one single breath for granted,
God forbid love ever leave you empty handed,
I hope you still feel small when you stand beside the ocean,
Whenever one door closes I hope one more opens,
Promise me that you'll give faith a fighting chance,
And when you get the choice to sit it out or dance.

I hope you dance . . . I hope you dance.

I hope you never fear those mountains in the distance,
Never settle for the path of least resistance
Livin' might mean takin' chances but they're worth takin',
Lovin' might be a mistake but it's worth makin',
Don't let some hell bent heart leave you bitter,
When you come close to sellin' out reconsider,
Give the heavens above more than just a passing glance,
And when you get the choice to sit it out or dance.

I hope you dance . . . I hope you dance.
I hope you dance . . . I hope you dance.
(Time is a wheel in constant motion always rolling us along, Tell me

who wants to look back on their years and wonder where those years have gone.)

I hope you still feel small when you stand beside the ocean,
Whenever one door closes I hope one more opens,
Promise me that you'll give faith a fighting chance,
And when you get the choice to sit it out or dance.

Dance . . . I hope you dance.[2]

---

2 *"I Hope You Dance."* Words and music by Mark D. Sanders and Tia Sillers. Copyright 2000. Soda Creek Songs/MCA Music Publishing Company. Used by permission.

About the Author

$\mathcal{J}$ elly Valimont is a national and international conference speaker whose passion is to see women in ministry fulfill their God-given roles. The pursuit of this passion leads Jelly to devote much of her time mentoring and training pastoral wives. Her "real life" approach to ministry has helped numerous pastors' wives realize that a complete and balanced ministry life is obtainable.

Jelly graduated from Southeastern University in Lakeland, Florida with a degree in Elementary Education and Bible. She has worked in the educational field in Florida, Arkansas, and Georgia both teaching school and as a school administrator.

In addition to teaching full-time, Jelly serves as the Administrative Consultant to the pastoral and support staff of Griffin First Assembly of God where she oversees all women's ministries and pastoral helps ministries.

Jelly is the wife of Senior Pastor, Randy Valimont, at First Assembly of God in Griffin, Georgia. She and her husband have been married for 29 years and have three daughters: Jordan, Danielle, and Alayna.

LaVergne, TN USA
01 November 2009
162685LV00005B/2/P